The Art of Papermaking

The Art
of Papermaking

Bernard Toale

Davis Publications, Inc.
Worcester, Massachusetts

Printed in the United States of America
Library of Congress Catalog Card Number: 82–74003
ISBN: 0-87192-140-5

Graphic Design: Donna Schenkel

10 9 8 7 6 5

Contents

Sheets, *Beverly Plummer, 1982. Hand beaten*
mulberry, cattail, and cabbage fiber. Photograph by
A. Hawthorne.

Acknowledgments

This book is the product of many people's labor. I particularly wish to thank Joanne Mattera for suggesting that I write it, and Wyatt Wade, my editor, for his support and sound judgment.

Sue Gosin and Paul Wong of Dieu Donne Press and Paper in New York City helped and encouraged me at every step. Sue and Paul also broadened the scope of the book by contributing a great deal of practical knowledge of the craft.

I wish also to thank Barbara Meirer-James and Jesse Munn, Lee McDonald, Lilian Bell, Tim Barrett, Mike Dorsa, Jane Farmer, Chris Guston, Winifred Lutz, and Lynn Forgach. The firsthand experience they shared was invaluable. Elaine Koretsky has been my sounding board, reference, and friend, and I am grateful for the many things she has taught me. Mr. and Mrs. B. J. Toale, my parents, have encouraged me throughout the project. Patty Fagan, alias Doctor Focus, is responsible for most of the black and white photography, and Gags Abbett drew the illustrations. Carolyn Scyocurka's hands at the typewriter made the manuscript legible, and her critical eye caught most of the errors.

This book is about craft and art, and I'm pleased to be able to show the work of so many fine artists. Without their innovations this book would be unnecessary. I am also grateful to all the writers about paper who came before me and eased my way.

I would be a small-town veterinarian today if it were not for Beverly Plummer, who questioned and supported me through all of the major decisions of my life. "It's your book!" she told me during one of my recent periods of doubt. Her inspiration and friendship has helped make it that.

And finally, I wish to thank Joe Zina for bearing with me through it all; without his support I never would have been able to do it.

The Art of Papermaking

Historically, people have written that paper is made in the beater. I would change that to read that durable and permanent papers with exceptional working characteristics are made through the careful choice of fibers, their controlled, gentle cooking, rinsing, and beating as well as skillful sheet forming. To these ends, and in the hope that the knowledge of these skills will lead people to produce quality sheet papers and beautiful, long lasting artworks, I dedicate this book.

1 | *History of Papermaking*

Papermaking in the European tradition. A Diderot Pictorial Encyclopedia of Trades and Industry, *1959.*

Paper has one history but two traditions, Oriental and European. Each is so different from the other that their products deserve two separate names, but both remain paper. Both traditions are based on the use of materials at hand, the working properties of these materials, and the writing implements and the development of printing processes within these cultures.

The process of macerating an assortment of vegetable fibers, floating them in water, collecting them on a screen, and allowing them to dry was first developed in China around 150 B.C. It produced a surface suitable for writing on with a brush and for woodblock printing, and the quantity produced was sufficient to meet the demands of the day.

The fibers for papermaking, the methods of production, and the resulting papers were studied intensely, and the craft was carried from China to Korea and then to Japan some 500 years later. These early papers were made from true hemp (*Cannabis sativa*). As the technology developed in Japan, three plants were discovered that produced thin, translucent papers of exceptional quality. The first and most common paper was made from the inner bark of the mulberry tree (*Broussonetia papyrifera*) and is known as kozo. Later, gampi and mitsumata were produced from the inner fibers of small, shrublike plants (*Wikstroemia canescens* and *Edgeworthia papyrifera*, respectively). During these formative years many other plants were tested, including bamboo, rice straw, linen, and banana. Recycling was also done to some degree to meet an ever growing demand for paper.

These prints show papermaking in the Oriental tradition. Kamisuki Chōhōki Kunisaki Jihei, *1798; reprinted by the University of California, Berkeley, California, 1948.*

The knowledge of papermaking traveled west along the trade routes to the Mediterranean. Early mills were established by Chinese prisoners in Samarkand in Central Asia around 750 A.D. The abundance of hemp and flax (*Linum usitatissimum*) in this area provided more fibers for papermaking, and the process spread to Egypt, where cotton, generally in the form of new cloth or rags, was added to the list of usable fibers. These new fibers produced papers that were thick, opaque, absorbent, and crisp, ideal for the existing writing tools, quill pens and styluses. And so, a new product developed, still called paper but looking very different than its ancestors. Papermaking moved across Europe, and in 1719 a French scientist, René de Reamur, observed that wasps made a very fine paper for their nests from wood digested in their mouths. With a shortage of cotton and linen cloth and an ever growing need for paper, this observation led to further plant experiments with nettles, moss, pine needles, and the barks of shrubs and trees.

It soon became apparent that whole trees, with extensive treatment, could produce paper. This new source of raw material led to the development of yet another technology and another class of papers. This group would no longer be made by hand. The quantity of pulp produced from a tree and the large demand for paper led to the invention of the Fourdrinier machine in 1806. It could produce paper on a continuous web and in enormous quantities. Hand papermaking came to the United States in 1690, but by the end of the American Civil War, modern industry, the use of the new papermaking machine, and the conversion to wood pulp effectively brought to an end the production of handmade paper in America.

The many layers of this wasp nest are made of paper.

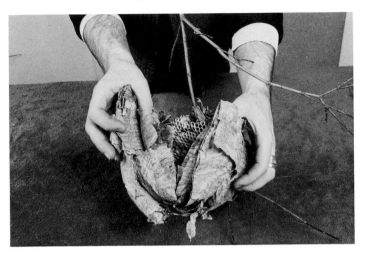

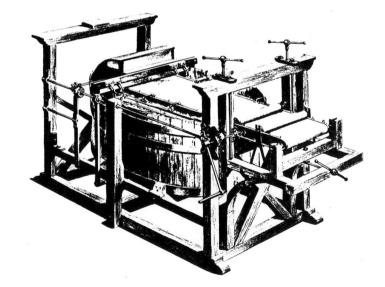

This is a model of the first papermaking machine, invented by Nicholas-Louis Robert in 1798.

The skill of making paper by hand, however, did not come to America to die. In 1928 Dard Hunter established a mill in Connecticut for producing hand sheets on a small scale, and his extensive research comprises most of today's reference material. He traveled around the world amassing a tremendous collection of hand papermaking equipment, materials, and samples of paper that are housed in The Dard Hunter Museum and Library at the Institute of Paper Chemistry in Appleton, Wisconsin.

The Papermaker, an in-house magazine of the Dupont Company, became the forum for many others interested in hand papermaking. Here in the 1950s and 60s Harrison Elliot, John Mason, and Henry Morris wrote extensively about their exploits, trials, and tribulations. Their writings provided humor and insight into this ancient craft and helped spark its revival.

Since 1946, Douglass Howell has continued his relentless exploration of flax fiber for use in hand sheets and for the production of paper art objects. And here began a new phase in the tradition of European papermaking, the paper art object. Oriental papers have always been used for kites, sliding screens, clothing, dolls, floor coverings, and in spiritual ceremonies. European papers have been the carriers of images or information, subservient to another medium. Now the stuff of paper, its color, its texture, its malleability, and its fibers are being used to accentuate their own inherent qualities. And artists are taking advantage of these qualities to create works that speak about image and paper, paper as image.

This Fourdrinier machine is able to produce forty-eight tons of lightweight paper a day. The sheets are 125 inches wide. Photo courtesy of Crane and Co., Dalton, Massachusetts.

Artwork by Douglass Howell.

Rock Series—In the Act of Shaking Hands,
Golda Lewis, 1979. 15½″ × 21½″.

The roots of this phenomenon can be traced to Laurence Barker and Garner Tullis, both of whom have shaped today's art-paper world. Barker studied briefly with Douglass Howell, then established a papermaking program at the Cranbrook Academy of Art in Bloomfield Hills, Michigan, in 1964. A printmaker by training, his many students learned papermaking based on good sheet formation and craftsmanship. Many of them have gone on to establish mills of their own. Garner Tullis learned papermaking in California more from industry than from a mentor and established the Institute for Experimental Printmaking in San Francisco. His approach breaks the rules, and in his work with other artists he has produced innovative two- and three-dimensional works—some of tremendous scale.

The hand mills of America today are not the mills of China or Europe or even of Dard Hunter's time. They are the products of these traditions but are heavily influenced by the needs of contemporary art. Artists can come to these mills to have custom archival sheets made for their books and work with mill technicians to produce two- and three-dimensional images from paper pulp. And these images may incorporate found objects, glitter, wire, resin, textile fragments, all of the materials of the working artist. While some artists are concerned with making art that will last forever, others use paper for temporary projects and spontaneous events. The medium today is alive and vibrant, proof that solid old traditions never die but are continually revitalized and born again in exciting new forms.

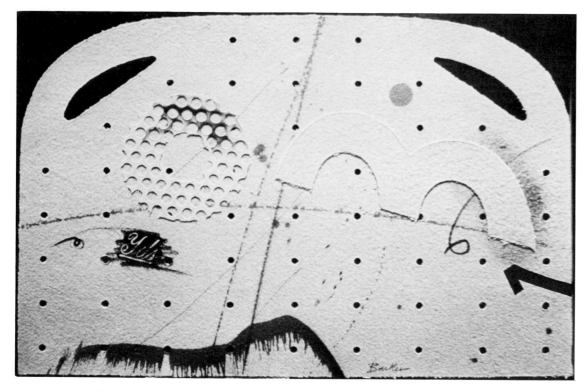

Laurence Barker, 1980. Cast and printed paper.

The Carriage House Handmade Paper Works in Brookline, Massachusetts, is one of the many professional facilities producing custom handmade papers and collaborative paper artworks. Elaine Koretsky, shown here, and her daughter, Donna, use the mill as a studio for creating their own artwork as well.

2 | *Oriental Papermaking*

A collection of Oriental papers.

The beauty of Oriental papers lies in their suppleness, transparency, surface qualities, and strength. This beauty does not come easily. The process is very laborious and time-consuming. To follow the tradition would mean growing the specific plants, harvesting, steaming, and stripping the bark from the woody core, separating the bark layers to obtain the usable fiber, cooking it, rinsing it, and beating it by hand into a pulp. The pulp would then be added to a vat of very cold water and formed into thin sheets. Traditionally, papermaking was a fall and winter activity. During the spring and summer, the land was farmed and the papermaking plants were grown. The cold weather also enhanced several working characteristics of the materials.

Fiber Sources

There are three main perennial plants grown for Oriental papermaking: kozo (*Broussonetia papyrifera*), mitsumata (*Edgeworthia papyrifera*), and gampi (*Wikstroemia canescens*). All three are classified as bast fibers. Each has its own characteristics and is used to make a specific kind of paper. All have long fibers that are easily separated during the cooking and beating process.

Kozo is a loosely applied term for a variety of papermaking mulberry trees. It is the most common of the three plants and is harvested after its second year of growth when the stems have reached a diameter of about one inch. It was one of the earliest cultivated plants used for paper and produces the toughest and strongest fibers. Its fibers are not very elastic, giving the resulting sheet great dimensional stability.

Mitsumata is harvested after its third year of growth and produces a soft, absorbent, fine-grained, slightly orange sheet. The fiber contains a bitter chemical that repels insects from papers produced with it.

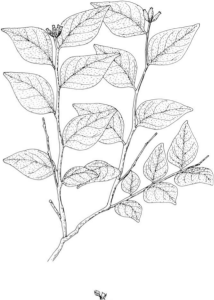

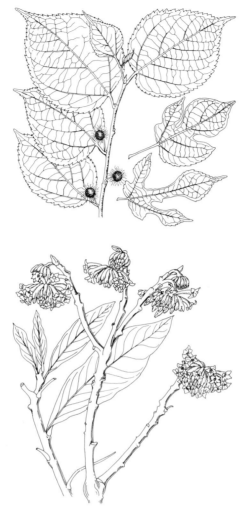

Kozo.

Mitsumata.

Gampi.

Hemp.

Gampi has never been successfully domesticated and consequently is not as readily available as kozo or mitsumata. Paper produced from gampi is reputed to be the most noble and beautiful of all and is said to be capable of lasting forever. It also repels insects.

Fiber produced by the hemp plant was used in China and was the most important papermaking material in early Japan, where it was gradually replaced by kozo. It produces a supple and strong sheet with a slightly rough surface.

Separating the Usable Fiber

Kozo, mitsumata, and gampi are harvested and cut to fit into steaming chambers—large covered wooden barrels or drums that rest over a wood fire. The steam causes the outer layer of the bark to swell. After two hours, the stalks are removed from the chambers and the outer layers are easily stripped from the hard woody core while the stalks are still hot. The stripped fiber is hung to dry in the sun for several days and then taken inside and stored for future papermaking. At this point it is called black bark because the dark outer bark remains on the inner layers of usable fibers, the green bark and white bark.

When the dried fiber is needed for papermaking, it is first soaked in cold running water for twenty-four hours to soften it and to loosen the black bark. This outer layer can be partially removed by walking on the bundles of fiber as they soak. The black bark is not fibrous and comes off in chips or flakes. The remainder is scraped off with a broad flat knife or other flat object. Paper made from partially or poorly cleaned fiber is called chiri-gami and is used for wrapping or waste paper in Japan or exported as a decorative paper.

After the black bark has been removed, the fiber is then soaked in cold running water for a day or placed in the sun or on the snow to gently bleach it. Once again it can be dried and stored or taken directly to be cooked.

Cooking the Fiber

The specifics of cooking are dependent more on family tradition, the desired product, and the conditions of the papermaker's life than on scientific guidelines. If a cooking pot is so big, it will hold so much pulp and water and to that you will need about so much caustic to dissolve unwanted parts of the plant. The ratio of caustic to fiber also will vary depending on the type of caustic used. Very mild caustics, such as wood ash or straw ash, might be used in the proportion of 30 to 100 grams of dry caustic to 100 grams of dry fiber, whereas only 20 grams of soda ash or 15 grams of lye might be needed to do a similar job.

When working with ashes, the dry material is placed in a basket. Sometimes the basket contains a layer of sand on the bottom which acts to filter large particles of ash. Water is poured over the ash and the liquid containing the dissolved caustic is collected and used as the cooking solution. The volume of water used determines the desired strength of the cooking solution. In attempting to duplicate this procedure it is advisable to rely on pH tests. A cooking solution with a pH of approximately 12 is needed to dissolve the noncellulose components of the plant in approximately two hours.

When the fiber has cooked for the desired time, it can be separated by gently pressing it between your fingers. The dark cooking solution containing the dissolved starches, sugars, and fats is washed away.

Gentle cooking in a mild caustic and thorough rinsings are extremely important to maintaining the inherent qualities and working properties of the fiber. Traditionally these cooked fibers were placed in a basket and rinsed in a stream for twenty-four hours to further brighten the fibers, which were then carefully reinspected for any traces of black bark.

Imported kozo fiber. This is the stripped green bark after the outer black bark has been removed.

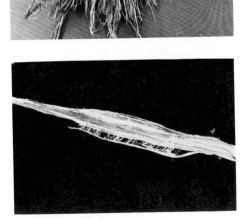

Even in its dry state, the fibrous nature of kozo green bark is apparent. After cooking, these long individual elements can be separated easily by hand beating.

Beating

These fibers are now ready to be separated from each other and hydrated by beating. A ball of fiber is placed on a wooden surface and beaten with hardwood mallets or rods until the individual fibrous elements have separated. This process takes between thirty minutes to one and a half hours. The fibers in the resulting pulp are extremely long and uncut, allowing for the production of thin papers of great strength and flexibility.

A Naginatta beater can also be used to separate the fibers. Its dull swordlike blades thrash through the already beaten pulp to separate it further.

The foot of the stamper beater rotates and macerates the damp fibers in the concrete basin.

Beating separates the softened fibers.

The design for this contemporary stamper beater for bast fibers is based on ancient Oriental equipment. It was built by Lee McDonald Papermaking Equipment for Winifred Lutz.

Mixing the Pulp

The vat in which the pulp is mixed should be large enough to accommodate the sheet-forming mold. A large wooden comblike device called a mase is used to stir the pulp solution but can be removed from the vat when it is not needed.

To the vat filled with cold water, prepared pulp is added and the contents are mixed. The ratio of pulp to water varies depending on the thickness and number of sheets being made. At this point a mucilaginous material called neri is added to the pulp and water. Neri comes from the root of the tororo-aoi plant (*Hibiscus manihot*), an annual plant that resembles okra and grows 12 to 18 inches high. Its thick and gnarled roots are collected before the first frost and stored. When beaten and soaked for several hours in cold water, they produce a thick mucilage that acts as a deflocculent, allowing long fibers to remain untangled in the vat and on the screen during sheet forming. The concentration of neri in the vat is determined more by feel and the sound of the water being stirred than by scientific proportion. This difficulty with accuracy is due in part to the viscosity of the neri, which is determined by the environment in which the plant is grown. A dry season, heavy rain, an early frost, too little fertilizer all affect the nature of the product (a synthetic neri also is available). This also holds true for the papermaking fibers themselves. As a rule, Oriental fiber plants grown in warmer climates will not produce as strong and lustrous a sheet as those grown in cooler temperatures. The slower growth rate of plants in cooler climates encourages the production of long, thin fibers from which exceptional paper is produced.

The mase rests in the upright supports on the vat and is used for stirring the pulp mixture. It can be removed after use.

The beaten pulp is added to the vat and thoroughly mixed using the mase.

Tororo-aoi.

Neri is added to the vat after the water and pulp.

The okra root can be pounded and soaked in cold water for several hours to produce a mucilage similar to that of tororo-aoi. This mucilage is strained through a cloth bag and added to the vat. Several pounds of okra root stock may be needed to produce enough neri for the production of one hundred sheets of paper.

Okra root.

Neri made from tororo-aoi, okra root, or synthetic neri must be kept cool—below 50°C—in order to maintain its extreme viscosity.

The viscosity of the water-neri mixture is greatly affected by temperature. As the temperature of the water rises, neri becomes less viscous, causing the pulp to drain too`quickly for proper sheet forming. Cold water also inhibits the growth of bacteria and fungus, which could break down the fibers and the neri in the vat as well as in the stack of final sheets in the slow pressing process.

The Mold

The frame for sheet forming consists of three parts: the ribbed mold; the removable surface, or su; and the deckle, which is usually hinged to the mold. This frame is strong and water-repellent, usually made of cypress wood, and is lightweight by comparison to its European counterpart, having only a few widely spaced ribs to support the screen surface. This structural difference is due primarily to three factors: the Oriental sheet-forming process does not involve the lifting and holding of large amounts of water; the mold surface of split bamboo or fine reed, twined together with silk thread, is lightweight and remains rigid when wet, requiring less support; and unlike the European method, in which the mold frame is used to transfer the newly-formed sheets onto absorbent blankets, only the su is used in the Oriental method.

Often large frames are fitted with handles set a comfortable distance apart and spanning across but above the forming surface. This allows the papermaker to form sheets larger than his or her normal reach. Production papermaking is a full-time job, so any improvements in the tools that make the process less strenuous and allow one to work longer hours are important. To this end frames are often attached by cords to a counterbalanced weight system, often as simple as flexible bamboo rods mounted in the ceiling, to aid in lifting the frame out of the water.

Overagitating the neri will reduce its effectiveness by reducing its viscosity.

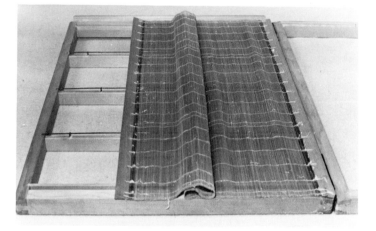

The deckle is hinged to the mold, and the flexible surface, the su, fits between them.

The su is sewn to two wedge-shaped pieces of wood that fit into notched counterparts in the mold when the deckle is closed. The su rests on wire supported above the ribs by pins.

Bamboo placemats can be modified for Oriental style sheet forming by covering them with a layer of gauze cloth. This helps to slow the drainage, prevents fibers from sticking to the bamboo, and gives the resulting sheet a smoother surface. This is based on a Japanese technique used when working with gampi fiber.

Sheet Forming

The sheet-forming process is called nagashi-zuki, or discharge papermaking. One of the significant differences between this and the European or sieve-type method is that the resulting sheet is the product of many laminations of extremely long-fibered pulp.

To form a sheet by the Oriental papermaking process, a small amount of long-fibered pulp and water is collected on the front edge of the mold. It is rolled back and forth across the mold in waves and then thrown off the back side of the mold. This process is repeated, each time accumulating more fibers on the mold surface, until the desired thickness is achieved. The hinged deckle is raised and the su, with its thin layer of pulp, is removed. This is laid, pulp side down, onto a wooden board or piece of woven cloth or felt. The su is gently pulled back from the sheet, which remains on the board or cloth, and is replaced in the mold to form the next sheet. Each successive sheet is laid directly on the previous wet sheet until a pile or post of several hundred sheets is formed. After pressing, these sheets will be separated from each other for drying.

The use of neri is critical to all stages of the sheet-forming process. It keeps long fibers untangled and evenly distributed in the vat. It increases the viscosity of the mixture, which slows its drainage through the su and gives the papermaker more time to align and orient the fibers. The increased viscosity also allows the papermaker to redip the mold many times in the vat, making a strong, laminated sheet. These characteristics allow one wet sheet to be placed on top of another wet sheet on the pile and prevent them from adhering to each other.

1

Pulp is collected on the front side of the mold and distributed over the su. The excess water is then discharged from the opposite side. Most of the water will be thrown off the mold and will not draw through the mold, as in the European style.

2

6

The mold rests on sticks that span the vat while the su is removed.

Several layers are laminated together by subsequent redipping of the mold. Each time, the fibers are distributed and aligned and the excess is thrown off with a flick of the wrists.

3

4

5

7

8

Layers of newly formed sheets of paper are laid on top of each other and allowed to drain or "weep" overnight, covered with a damp cloth or felt.

9

The stack of newly formed sheets is allowed to stand overnight before being pressed. During this period water and neri gently seep out of the stack. In fact, in the final dried sheet of paper there is virtually no trace of neri. It is unclear whether it becomes another compound or its viscous nature pulls it all out of the sheets as one unit.

Pressing

The Oriental press can be a very simply constructed machine. In its most simple form it can be several large rocks placed on a board on top of the stack of paper. Others can be simple levers made from tree trunks with the stack of paper as the fulcrum. Hydraulic and screw presses are also used.

Gentle pressing is extremely important to prevent the fresh sheets from sticking to each other. The sheets are usually left in the press for twelve hours, and the pressure is increased gradually during this time.

Drying

After the sheets are removed from the press, they are carefully separated from each other in the stack and brushed onto large drying boards with wide horsehair brushes. These boards are then carried out into the sun to dry and, depending on the weather, the paper is peeled off and ready for use in one hour or less. This process can be shortened even further by brushing the papers onto heated metal plates. This creates a very smooth surface on the side of paper in contact with the metal plate and makes the paper more crisp than when it is board dried.

Most Oriental papers are absorbent. If a less porous, smoother surface is needed, a small percentage of kaolin, china clay, ground sea shell, or rice powder may be added to the pulp mixture. The finished paper can also be rubbed with a smooth stone or leaf to polish its surface.

The stack of papers on a board is placed in the press. This press, modified by Tim Barrett of Kalamazoo Handmade Papers, is based on an ancient Oriental design. By adding water to a bucket, pressure can be gradually increased over a twelve-hour period. Oriental papers are pressed at approximately 18 pounds per square inch, as opposed to 150 pounds per square inch for European papers.

A closer view of the top of the press.

An assortment of brushes can be used to press the sheets to the boards.

After twelve hours, the papers are separated, or "parted," from the stack. Each pulp reacts differently at parting. The sheets in a "dry" stack may bond together. Those in a wet stack may tear easily. Fine reeds or threads may be added along the edge of each sheet when forming the stack to aid in separating them later. The separated sheets are brushed onto a flat surface, of wood or metal, to dry. When dry, the sheets are peeled away from the board.

Decorative Effects

The process of lamination and the production of thin, strong, translucent papers allows the papermaker many options for decorative effects. Plant material other than the bast fiber can be added to the vat to give the resulting sheets additional visual and textural interest. Larger flat objects, such as leaves, metal foil, butterfly wings, and flower petals, can be placed on the surface of a wet sheet and embedded in the sheet by redipping the mold in the vat. The transparent nature of this thin lamination allows the objects to be clearly revealed in the dried paper. If a stencil of treated paper or thin metal is placed over a freshly made sheet and sprayed with a fine mist of water, the droplets will distort the fibers of the sheet. When the stencil is removed, the image or pattern will appear as a thin area in the sheet, creating a lacelike effect. This thin sheet can be used alone or placed on top of another sheet of dyed paper to enhance its image. Stencils can be used in other ways. Metal frames, like cookie cutters, can be placed on the newly formed sheet and colored fibers in water poured into them.

The colored fibers can be pressed on the surface, or the sheet can be redipped to seal them within the sheet. Colored fibers in a tororo-aoi and water mixture can be poured over the wet base sheet to create bands of thin colors that when overlapped create more colors. The surface quality of the sheet can also be affected by mixing fibers of different lusters and textures. The redipability in Oriental sheet-forming makes it a fertile field for artistic exploration.

The dried paper can be dyed by several traditional techniques. Because of its great strength, it can be folded, twisted, and rewetted. Folding and tie-dyeing are two common methods for coloring the finished paper. Wax or paste-resist techniques also can be used.

Washi, the term for Japanese paper, has influenced every aspect of traditional Japanese life, from what is worn to how light enters the house. The beauty and versatility of this material is unsurpassed, and the time and effort required to produce it enrich the maker.

The Geometric Kimono Suite, *Sandy Kinnee. 22¼" × 28". Intaglio on handmade rag paper. Photographs by Dick Robinson.*

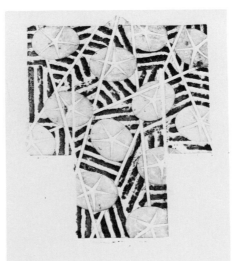

Camouflage, *Susan Lyman. 11¾" × 19" × 19". Reed, bamboo, straw paper, plaster gauze, and varnish.*

Gomer, *Suzanne Ferris. 10" × 72". A book collaboration with Neal Bonham, potter, and Mark Halpern, poet.*

Reef Dwelling, *Joan Austin, 1980. 8″ × 8″. Cast pulp, enamel, and pigment.*

Winocia, *Barbara Schwartz, 1980. 59″ × 63″ × 14″. Casein on handmade paper over wire lath screen.*

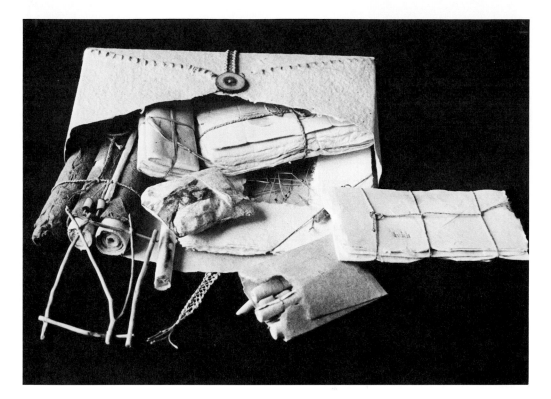

The Ancient Mariner Series, The Primrose,
*Robert Nugent, 1978. 11½″ × 15″ × 2¾″. Hand-
made rag and mulberry papers, wood, bone, raffia,
conte, nineteenth-century English letters, sea ur-
chin spine, and hemp. Courtesy of Grapestake Gallery, San Francisco.*

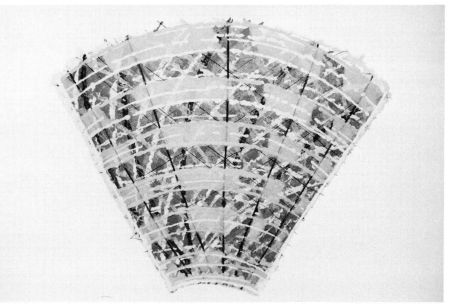

Fan #50: Collingwood, *Czashka Ross, 1982. 30″
× 36″. Linen, silk threads, ribbon, and stainless
steel.*

3 | Papermaking from Plants

Each kind of plant will produce paper with its own inherent characteristics.

A sheet of paper is close to one hundred percent cellulose, and all plants contain cellulose. Knowing this, the variety of papermaking fibers is as broad as the whole plant kingdom. Many plants have been tested for their papermaking qualities, and the results are part of industry or tradition. Some have been found unsuitable for large-scale manufacturing because they require very special handling or the percentage of usable fiber from the bulk of the plant is too small. All plants, however, offer the artist and hand papermaker a wide range of unique pulps. Each will produce paper with a distinct color, texture, and transparency, and most of these papers will cost absolutely nothing but the time required to harvest and process the plants. To find a specific plant, research it, process it, and make sheets from it puts the whole process on a very intimate, personal level and gives each sheet of paper an added importance.

There are several ways to approach the search for usable plant fibers. The first is to walk out the back door with a scissors and brown bag in hand and start cutting. You can't really go wrong. A second approach would be to examine the plants that are now being used and study historical fiber research. There are certain plant families that produce fiber used in the textile and paper industry. Many of these plant families are quite broad and you will often find members growing in your area. For example, in the same family as cotton, a traditional papermaking fiber, you will also find okra and hollyhock. There is a wide geographical distribution of many related plants all having similar characteristics. The mulberry tree used for papermaking in Japan will produce different results from the mulberry in your back yard, but the one in your back yard is yours and free and will produce a unique and beautiful sheet.

Helmut Becker harvests fiber flax, which he grows for paper pulp.

Iris and lily leaves, okra, hollyhock bast, cornstalks, and bulrushes are among the many native plants that can be used to make paper.

The search for papermaking fibers has been a continuous one since the development of the process. The paper produced from your iris leaves or the weeds that grow between the cracks in the sidewalk will add to this knowledge and broaden your perspective on the search. Another advantage to this type of papermaking is that processing these materials requires only a minimum of equipment.

Suitable plants for papermaking can be divided into three categories: bast, leaf, and grass. Seed fibers (cotton, milkweed, and kapok) and wood also can be used but are more difficult to process by hand.

Bast Fibers

Bast fibers are those collected from the inner bark or phloem, the transportation tissue of the plant through which water is supplied to the plant and food produced in the leaves is carried to be stored in the roots. Bast fibers are long, slender, and strong and can be hand beaten to produce translucent, dense sheets. Some plants, such as okra, can be stripped of their bast fibers while still green due to a mucilaginous substance that holds these fibers from the woody core. Others, such as kudzu, are easily separated from the core of the plant by the Oriental steaming and stripping method. This method can also be applied to any branch or yearly growth of any tree or shrub. Elm trees, lilac, and privet bushes as well as mulberry can be tested. The bast fibers of herbaceous plants like milkweed, flax, okra, or true hemp can be removed by a process called retting, a slow bacterial cooking method. This can be done in two ways. The simplest is to allow the cut plant to lie in the field exposed to the weather for a period of time after it is harvested. Bacterial activity and the effect of rain and sun will partially deteriorate noncellulose components of the plant, making it

easier to remove the bast fiber by stripping or pounding. The second method involves more control over the bacterial activity and the state of dampness of the fibers. Milk or beer is added to water containing the harvested plants, and the plants are stirred frequently for one to several weeks, depending on the types of plants, the temperature of the air (warm weather increases bacterial activity), and the bacterial activity. When the fibers can be easily separated from the stalk, the plants are removed from the tank and rinsed, and the fibers are stripped, rinsed again, and beaten or further cooked.

Bast fibers can be removed from the inner bark of the branches and young growth of such perennial plants as birch, hazelnut, red cedar, acacia, wisteria, mulberry, linden, fig, eucalyptus, and willow. It can be found and removed from such annual plants as flax, nettle, burdock, milkweed, thistle, dogbane, kudzu, hollyhock, okra, and true hemp. Many of these plants have been used for the production of cordage and cloth and for papermaking. Most are commercially unavailable and must be harvested and processed by the papermaker.

Leaf Fibers

Leaf fibers are shorter and more opaque than bast fibers and generally produce a paper with a rougher texture. They are often used in the box industry and for making heavyweight card stock. Many leaf fibers (sisal, pineapple, yucca) need to be scraped to remove their tough, water-repellent outer layer before cooking or retting. Many have been used for cordage and textiles and several (sisal, Manila hemp, raffia) can be purchased at local hardware and weaving supply stores.

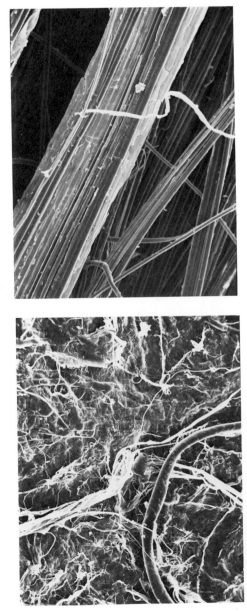

This scanning electron photomicrograph of flax fiber magnified 200 times shows long, straight fibers held in bundles. Cooking and beating will separate these into individual elements. Courtesy of Helmut Becker.

This view of a sheet of paper made from flax fiber, magnified 200 times, shows how the individual elements flatten together to form a tight web.

In these controlled retting tanks, various plant parts are soaked and turned often to expose them to the air. As the soft tissue of the plant begins to deteriorate, it reveals the usable fiber bundles that will later be freed by rinsing.

The stalks are cut to a manageable length for steaming. Although taller than the pot, these can be wrapped in a tent of aluminum foil and then cloth to retain the heat. This pot contains okra, milkweed, and hollyhock stems, which will be steamed for about one-half hour or until the bast easily separates from the stalk.

After lying in the field for a month or more, this lustrous white milkweed fiber is easily removed from the stalk.

While still hot, the okra bast is easily stripped away.

The scraped okra bast fiber can be sun bleached and dried for future use or processed immediately for sheet forming. Cooking in a mild caustic for two hours and hand beating after thoroughly rinsing will produce a light, cream-colored pulp suitable for sheet forming. According to Lilian Bell, in Plant Fibers for Papermaking, *the* Mobile Register *was printed on okra paper in 1870.*

The outer bark can then be scraped off with a flat bladed tool, such as a putty knife, and can be discarded or used later as decoration in the paper.

Fiber Lengths

Bast fibers

Ramie	120 mm
Nettle	19–80 mm
Milkweed	10–45 mm
Flax	33 mm
Hemp (true)	25 mm
Kozo	10 mm
Jute	1–5 mm
Mitsumata	3 mm
Gampi	3 mm
Okra	2.43 mm

Leaf fibers

Sisal	3–7 mm
Pineapple	3–7 mm
Abaca (textile banana)	3–7 mm
Sansevieria	2 mm
Raffia	1–2 mm

Grass fibers

Bamboo	1–5 mm
Corn husk and stalk	1–5 mm
Papyrus	1–4 mm
Sugar cane	1.5–2.7 mm

Source: Lilian Bell, *Plant Fibers for Papermaking*, McMinnville, Oregon: Liliaceae Press, 1981.

"Fiber lengths vary from one fiber type to another, as well as within a particular plant. Fiber *width*, although not noted, also varies. A thicker fiber gives a coarser paper while a thinner fiber results in a more flexible, smoother paper that offers a better printing surface" (Lilian Bell, in *Plant Fibers for Papermaking*).

Grass Fibers

Grasses produce the shortest and most brittle papermaking fibers. The yield per volume of dry fiber is also low, but their geographic distribution is so broad and their availability so great that they should not be overlooked. Many are hollow stemmed and buoyant in water, which makes them difficult to cook. Some, like cornstalks and bamboo, can be split with a knife or crushed with a mallet, then cut into usable pieces for cooking. Bulrushes, beach grass, sugar cane, wheat, and rice straw can all be used, and many others are traditional papermaking fibers. Bamboo is still used widely in China and to a limited extent in Japan.

The plants in the families Thymelaceae, Moreceae, Musaceae, Gramineae, and Liliaceae will provide you with a good starting point when examining botanical reference books. These families are broad and contain known papermaking plants.

Cooking the Fibers

Once the plants have been collected, they must be cooked to remove extraneous material, sugars, starch, wax, and lignin. If these were left in the plant, they would inhibit beating and proper separation of the fibers. They also decompose more rapidly than cellulose and would cause the resulting sheet to yellow and become brittle with age. With Oriental, European, and local plant fibers, a mild caustic cooking solution can be used to reveal the inherent characteristics of the specific fibers and remove unwanted materials. With such a broad range of plants, growing conditions, harvesting, and preprocessing possibilities, it is difficult to give any specific directions for cooking other than to be gentle. Simmering in a 1 percent caustic solution for two hours usually will result in undamaged fibers. Some will require longer cooking times as well as a second cooking. Because of the many variables in working with organic materials, it is best to observe carefully and record your results. *Plant Fibers for Papermaking*, by Lilian Bell, is an excellent reference book for those interested in working with local plants. She recommends one tablespoon of lye or washing soda for each quart of water.

The following table will be helpful in determining the caustic to use and in what proportion. The pH scale is used to determine the acidity and alkalinity of a substance. The numbers of the scale range from 0 (strong acid) to 14 (strong base), with 7 being neutral.

10 grams of caustic in 1 liter of neutral pH water equals 1% solution

15 grams of caustic in 1 liter of neutral pH water equals 1.5% solution

20 grams of caustic in 1 liter of neutral pH water equals 2% solution

Common Name	Chemical Name	pH at 1%	pH at 1.5%	pH at 2%
Lye or caustic soda	Sodium hydroxide	13.4	13.5	13.7
Washing soda, soda ash	Sodium carbonate	11.5	11.6	11.8
Wood ash	Potassium carbonate	11.4	11.5	11.6

Be advised that these caustics can cause skin irritations. Rubber gloves, aprons, protective eye covering, and a well-ventilated room are strongly recommended.

Strong caustics speed cooking but can make the usable fibers brittle. The resulting sheets may have a rougher surface and be less strong than if the fiber had been prepared in a weaker caustic and cooked for a longer period.

After cooking, the fibers must be thoroughly rinsed to remove all traces of the cooking solution. The pH of the cooked fiber should be tested. This can be done with disposable pH test strips available at most drugstores. Place the strip on the wet fiber and compare it to the color scale that comes with the kit. The pH of thoroughly washed fibers should be close to neutral.

Bleaching the Fibers

All fibers have their own unique, inherent color. The color can be used as is or lightened by several bleaching methods. Exposing the cooked fibers to sunlight or placing them in cold running water for twenty-four hours will brighten them. Care should be taken that they do not become moldy or contaminated during these processes. Chemical bleaching agents can be used; hydrogen peroxide is the safest. Fibers in a hydrogen peroxide and water solution will brighten in several days, and the hydrogen peroxide will not leave any residue on the fiber. Commercially available chlorine laundry bleaches should be avoided if permanence of the finished paper is important. Although these bleaches act very quickly, the residual chlorine in the fiber will eventually lead to the oxidation of the cellulose and cause the paper to become brittle and yellow. If chlorine must be used, the fibers should then be soaked for twenty-four hours in a calcium carbonate or magnesium carbonate solution (50 grams of carbonate to 1 liter of water) to thoroughly buffer the chlorine. Since other bleaching methods are available, it seems wise to avoid chlorine bleaches altogether.

Beating the Fibers

Many plant pulps can be hand beaten by the Oriental method. Place the damp fibers on a hard surface and beat them with a wooden mallet or club. An oak board, two inches by four inches by eighteen inches, shaped at one end to form a handle, works well. The beating time will vary with each plant from one-half hour to several hours. To test if the fibers have separated, place a small amount in a glass of water and shake thoroughly. Hold this up to a light and examine the suspension carefully. If it is without clumps or knots and appears as small, fine, individual fibers, the process is finished.

Commercial blenders will hold up to one gallon of pulp.

A kitchen blender can be used to beat cooked plant fibers. Here, iris leaves are being cut into small sections. Cooked for two hours in a mild caustic, rinsed, blended, and sheet formed, the fibers will produce lustrous, light tan sheets of paper.

Ball mills can be used to separate small quantities of pulp. Photograph by Lilian Bell. Courtesy of Liliaceae Press.

A Hollander beater can prepare large quantities of pulp.

Time is a factor that cannot be overlooked in any hand process. The pleasure of collecting and processing plants can be quickly overshadowed if it takes two days to hand beat the fiber into usable pulp, which could be the case with flax. The electric kitchen blender or a ball mill used in ceramic and lapidary studios can be used to shorten this time. Plant parts should be cut into one-half inch lengths before being placed in the blender to avoid entanglement in the blades. The percentage of fiber to water should be small, one-quarter cup of fiber to a blender full of water. Blending time will vary from a few seconds to several minutes, depending on the fiber. To beat fibers in a ball mill, add one ounce of dry fiber and five pounds of porcelain beads to the one and one-quarter gallon porcelain jar of the ball mill. This jar rests on a rotating stand, and as it turns the pebbles roughen and separate the fiber. The ball mill works best on longer leaf fibers such as sisal and iris and on some bast fibers. The jar rotates from one to six hours. The disadvantage of these two machines, and particularly the ball mill, is that only a small amount of fiber can be processed at one time.

When large amounts of cooked fiber are to be beaten, the Hollander beater, used in European papermaking, can be used. This machine consists of a rotating roller and bedplate, which are mounted in a circular trough filled with water. As the roller turns, it separates the fibers. Most small Hollander beaters can process approximately one pound of fiber at a time.

A simple, durable mold can be made using a plastic grid as the support system, hardware cloth as an underwire, and a finer wire on the top surface. The frame can be made of pine, glued with a water-resistant glue, and nailed at the corners. All of these materials are available at local hardware stores or lumberyards.

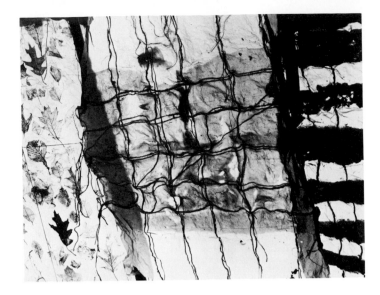

Solar Snow House, *Helmut Becker, 1982. 9' ×
13'. Bleached fiber flax, leaves, seaweed, netting,
yarn, and stainless steel.*

Solar Long House (detail), *Helmut Becker, 1980.
A variety of plants and textile materials have been
incorporated in this sculptural work.*

Rock Edifice, *Judith Sugarman. 34″ × 5′. By pressing newly formed cotton sheets onto a rock surface and allowing them to dry, this highly textured surface was created. It was later treated with colored pigment.*

Untitled, *Pat Warner. 50″ × 60″ × 14″. The translucent nature of flax paper is emphasized in this work, which also incorporates thistle and rag fibers.*

1

The fibrous pulp is mixed in a vat of water.

The frame or deckle is placed over the screen-covered mold.

2

5

After a few seconds of draining, the deckle can be removed.

6

The freshly formed sheet will adhere to the screen and can be pressed on a cloth surface. This cloth, or felt, can be an old blanket or other absorbent textile and should be thoroughly wet before use. A wet cloth will hold the new sheet better than a dry one.

The mold is passed under the water.

3

The mold is raised, and the collected fibers are gently shaken to align them.

4

7

Pressing on the back of the mold will cause the pulp to stick to the cloth. This process is called couching.

8

Lifting the mold will reveal the new sheet.

Shaped papers are easily formed by changing the shape of the deckle. Here Masonite sealed with polyurethane is used as a deckle.

1

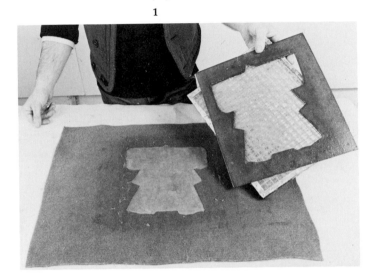

Openings in the sheet can be produced by adhering masking tape to the surface of the mold.

2

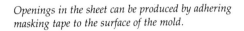

4

Other pulps can be applied by squeezing them from plastic squirt bottles. Pressing will flatten the pulp and bond the fibers. If flatness is not desired, a small amount of adhesive (methylcellulose) can be added to the pulp to assure the bonding of the fibers and the work can be left unpressed to air dry.

5

Here Roland Cook pours pulp into sections of a metal frame placed on top of an unpressed sheet. The frame is removed before the paper is pressed.

Objects can be embedded between two fresh sheets.
Pressing this will bond the two layers together and
embed added materials.

3

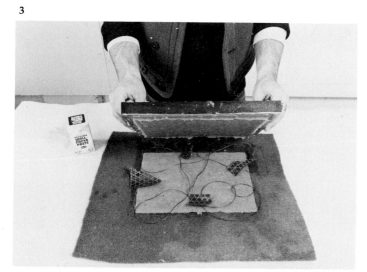

After a minute or so in the press, the paper can be
removed, picked up, and brushed onto a smooth
surface to dry. It can also be transferred to another
dry felt, re-pressed, and then left to dry in the air
or on a flat window screen.

7

6

Pressing can be done in a simple book press or by
placing a board over the felts and bricks or other
heavy objects on the board. Extra felts should be in-
cluded to help absorb the water.

The Island of Jump, *Joel Carreiro. 30" × 144".*
Pigment on shaped, handmade paper.

Untitled, *Pat Warner. 31" × 30" × 10". Flax,*
rag, and thistle paper were used to create this
translucent work.

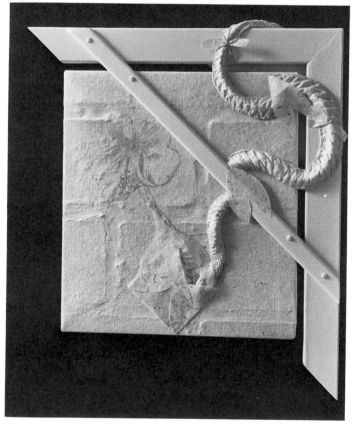

Fragments: Visual/Tactile Book XII, *Trudy Guinee, 1980. 9½" × 5½" × 1". This multiple-couched piece includes fragments of cotton, linen, jute, plant parts, gauze, bark, color Xerox photographs, dye, and pencil drawings.*

Veiled Threats, *Lilian Bell. 14" × 16" × 3". Milkweed, gampi, and redwood fibers were used in this cast piece.*

This electron photomicrograph shows corn husk fiber in a paper sample magnified 130 times. The fiber for this paper was prepared in the ball mill. Photomicrograph by Tony Bell. Courtesy of Liliaceae Press.

Papermaking from Old Papers

Another category of pulps to consider are those made by reprocessing old papers. Because the original paper has been dried and probably printed and drawn on, the resulting paper will have a different character than the original but is an excellent source of inexpensive pulp for many uses. The original paper should always be considered before starting. High-grade cotton drawing and printing papers and glossy photographic magazine papers are good for some uses. These papers should be cut into small pieces (one-inch square or smaller) and soaked for twenty-four hours in water. After rinsing, the pulp may be cooked in a mild caustic solution for two hours to further clean and soften it. Rinsed again, it can be beaten in a blender or a Hollander beater. Expect these papers to have unique characteristics. Some will make good pulps for sheet forming and others will be good for sculptural works. Some, like lightly blended magazine photographs, can be added to more stable pulps for decorative effects. It is also a good idea to buffer these pulps, by soaking them in a calcium carbonate or a magnesium carbonate solution, owing to their unknown, original treatment and processing. This can be done by mixing 50 grams of carbonate with each liter of water and soaking the pulp overnight.

Each pulp will have its own physical as well as visual characteristics. Some will drain very slowly on the mold and others will drain fast. Some will produce papers with smooth surfaces and others will be rough. Some will dye bright and lustrous and others will be opaque and matte. By blending these together, pulps can be developed to satisfy your personal aesthetic need.

Documentation of Papermaking from Plants
There are several things to consider when exploring and documenting a pulp. There is no bad pulp. There are bad applications of pulp. Thorough testing and record keeping will help avoid some mistakes.

(1) Its average fiber length; this affects strength.
(2) How it was cooked, the ratio of caustic to water, the cooking and rinsing times, and the amount of dry fiber used. These factors affect many characteristics of the paper.
(3) How it is beaten: by hand, electric blender, or Hollander beater.
(4) Its drainage rate on the mold.
(5) The surface characteristics of the resulting sheet, its texture, and whether the surface is easily damaged by picking with a pin.
(6) Its density and transparency.
(7) How much it shrinks when drying.
(8) Its color.
(9) How it might be treated or used with another pulp.

A sample record chart might look something like this.

Common name	Scientific name	Average fiber length
Cooking—caustic and percentage	Cooking time	Rinsing time
Beating method	Beating time	
Mold used	Drainage rate	
Felts used	Couching	
Drying procedure		

Paper Characteristics

Color	Surface
Strength (folding)	Transparency

Size:

Wet	Air dried	Blotter dried

Possible uses

Historical reference

4 | *European Papermaking*

A Hollander beater operator at Gandhi Ashram, Ahmedabad, India, preparing cotton rag pulp. Photograph courtesy of Lynn Forgach, Exeter Press, 1982.

Traditional European Papermaking

Traditional European papers are most often seen in old books and documents. They have a warm white color that contrasts with the crisp black type impressed in their surface. They have a supple feel and drape when the book is opened. The surface shows the texture of the woolen blankets on which the newly formed sheets are pressed, and the edges of the sheets have a slight cockle or wave. The edge itself is not sharp as if cut from a larger piece but is slightly irregular and is referred to as deckled. These white papers were made from linen and cotton fiber that came to the papermill in the form of new cloth or rags. These were dampened and rolled into balls, and the balls were allowed to ferment for up to two months. This fermenting was actually a slow cooking process that softened the fibers. After rinsing, the cloth fragments were placed in the basin of a mechanical stamper, and a heavy wooden hammer or shaft powered by a waterwheel rose and fell on the softened material to separate its fibers. The stamping process did not involve cutting, so the resulting pulp was long-fibered and supple, producing papers of great beauty, strength, and durability.

The time-consuming stamping process was slowly replaced by the invention of the Hollander beater. In its oblong-shaped tub was a roller fitted with metal blades, which lacerated the rags as they passed between it and a stone bedplate mounted in the bottom of this tank. This machine could process rag in much less time, but the resulting fiber had been cut shorter and produced a paper with less suppleness and strength.

A sheet of paper is not held together by magic or by simply piling fibers on top of one another. The bonding or cohesion of surfaces of cellulose within the fiber sheet is not due to a mucilage or glue either but to an electrochemical process in which hydrogen bonds form between the fibers. These fibers are drawn together and aligned by the presence of liquid water during the sheet-forming process. Water is the medium for the activity, and as it is removed during the draining, pressing, and drying of the sheet, it produces tension that draws the fibers together. This bonding of the fibers is aided by fibrils, which are small, hairlike abrasions on the surface of each fiber, caused during the beating process. These increase the surface texture of the fibers and consequently increase friction between fibers. This friction as well as the physical interlocking of the fiber during sheet forming aid in the bonding of the sheet. Other factors that affect cohesion are the average length of the individual fibers, their flexibility, and the degree of fibrillation on their surfaces. These components can be altered by the cooking and beating method used to prepare the fiber.

Cellulose is a hydrophilic (water-loving) carbohydrate composed of a molecular glucose chain of up to 5,000 units. It is found in varying degrees in all plants, but for the European papermaker the most easily reclaimed fibers came from the seed hairs of cotton and in the bast fiber of flax. By using woven textiles, much of the time-consuming preprocessing of the raw fiber was eliminated at the mill.

Other components of the plant also affect papermaking, particularly lignin and hemicellulose. Lignin is often referred to as an intercellular cement. It holds the fiber bundles together in the plant. It is hydrophobic (water-fearing) and must be removed by cooking. Its presence in the pulp reduces fiber separation during beating and interfiber bonding during sheet forming.

Hemicellulose has quite the opposite effect. It lies on the surface and is more hydrophilic than cellulose. It makes a pulp more susceptible to fibrillation during beating and makes the beaten fiber more flexible. The presence of both of these components in a pulp is affected by the nature of the specific fiber and how it is cooked. Overcooking can weaken the cellulose and dissolve the lignins and hemicellulose, making the fiber brittle and the resulting paper less strong.

With the invention of the Hollander beater, cooking was often eliminated. This machine can actually cut the fibers so the need to soften them beforehand was reduced. Today, cooking cotton cloth in small handmills is seldom done. Natural-colored linen is sometimes cooked to remove waxes and pectin and to lighten its color.

The main effects of processing fiber in the Hollander beater are to increase external fibrillation, increase internal fibrillation, and shorten or cut the fiber length. A properly prepared pulp can be made into a variety of papers, from soft and opaque to thin and translucent, depending on the manner in which it is beaten.

Cotton seed fibers and bast fiber bundles lie more or less parallel to the direction in which the plant grows. The Hollander beater mechanically separates these bundles into fine, long, individual fibrous threads, which are then bruised and abraded to expose even finer fibrils on the surface of each fiber. Because of the hydrophilic nature of cellulose, these fibers and fibrils immediately attract water molecules to themselves and form a layer or temporary envelope around them. This envelope acts as a lubricant and allows the tiny fibers to more easily interweave with each other during sheet formation. This physical interlocking aided by fibrillation is one of the ways paper is held together. A successful beating operation is one in which many fibers and fibrils are separated and enveloped in water, a process called hydration.

Papermaking fibers are hollow tubes of cellulose. The extent to which the inside of this tube is fractured determines the flexibility of the fiber. A more flexible fiber will interweave more completely and will be compacted more easily during sheet forming and pressing. These internal fibers will also aid in the collapse of the fiber, turning it into a flattened ribbon in the final sheet and making that paper dense and strong.

In addition to causing external and internal fibrillation, beating produces fines, thin membranes or small chunks of fiber that remain mixed with fibrillated pulp. These act as fillers; they fill in spaces between the overlapping, longer fibers and help to improve the smoothness of the surface of the sheet. They also slow the passage of water through the web of fibers during sheet forming. This slower drainage allows the papermaker more time to align the fibers on the papermaking mold.

After beating, the pulp is transferred to a storage chest or put directly into the forming vat. Historically, these European vats were built over small fireplaces. These fires heated the water and pulp. Since warm water is less viscous than cold and does not cling to the fiber as well, sheets formed in warm water drain faster, allowing the papermaker to make more sheets in a day.

The European sheet-forming method requires the lifting and holding of large amounts of water. Consequently, the molds developed for this are much more substantial than the Oriental ones, having an elaborate system of ribs that hold the wire surface level. This level surface aids in the formation of an even sheet and aids drainage. It can be a woven, noncorrosive wire mesh or a series of laid wire rods twined together.

A production mill setup consists of one deckle and two molds for each size of paper being made. The papermaker forms a sheet, sets it aside to drain and removes the deckle which he or she places on the second mold. While the papermaker forms the second sheet, his or her assistant presses the first mold onto a woolen blanket called the felt. The transfer of the sheet from the mold to the felt is called couching. Another felt is placed on top of the newly formed sheet, the mold is given back to the papermaker, and the process continues. These felts act as spacers between the wet sheets, allowing the water to move away quickly from the paper during pressing. A pile of papers and felts, called a post, is built up to a given height and put into the press.

The press can be either manual or hydraulic and serves two functions. It changes pulp into paper by dramatically reducing its water content to the point where hydrogen bonding can begin. This first pressing also decreases the thickness of the sheet and, by compacting its fibers, increases its strength. Pulp would become paper if left to dry unpressed, but pressing speeds this process and makes it stronger.

Etching of a drying loft from A Diderot Pictorial Encyclopedia of Trades and Industry.

Traditionally, after pressing, the sheets were put together in groups of six to ten and lightly pressed together to form a unit called a spur. These sheets temporarily bonded together and were taken to dry in a room in which the atmosphere was carefully controlled. Here they were laid on flat screened frames or hung over horsehair ropes and allowed to dry slowly. When dry, the sheets were separated from each other and re-pressed to remove any distortions that invariably occurred.

Although the sheets now appeared dry, they were still not ready for market. Aging allowed the fibers to shrink slowly and the paper to reach its final state of dryness and achieve dimensional stability. Most handmade writing and printing papers were then sized with an animal glue. This sizing made the paper less absorbent, protected it from abrasions, and made it stronger. After a second drying and aging period, these papers were ready for use. A testament to the ancient papermaker's art is that many old books and manuscripts still survive today with their information carried on a strong, flexible surface of paper.

Contemporary Papermaking

Contemporary papermaking is not the craft of history. Many innovations have been made in allied fields and in our lifestyles that make the process new again. Industries have been established that bring a wide range of precooked pulps to our door, central heating has eliminated the need for woodstoves under the vats, and drying machines have been devised that dramatically reduce drying times. Because of these changes, a thorough understanding of the process, its tools, and equipment are needed to help the new papermaker make intelligent choices when confronted with the range of decisions involved in starting a new mill, a small studio, or in working with pulp in a classroom.

Water Quality

An extremely important consideration in papermaking is water quality. Water is involved in every step of the process, from soaking the cloth through cooking, beating, and sheet forming. Even as a sheet dries, any mineral or organic residue in the water will migrate to the surface and mar it. The permanence of a sheet of paper is dramatically affected by these impurities as well.

Water can be tested by municipal water departments, agricultural agencies, or water filter salesmen. Pure water is a neutral liquid having a pH of 7.0. Trapped gases (chlorine and fluoride) and dissolved metals (copper, iron, and manganese) alter the pH of water and make it acidic (less than 7.0). Cellulose decomposes by oxidation in an acidic solution, causing paper to become brittle and yellow in color.

These trapped gases, dissolved metallic salts, and organic particles can be removed by filtering systems. There are two types of filters on the market, one removes particles, and the other removes dissolved salts. Both can be equipped with cartridges that contain charcoal, and both will then remove trapped gases. Recent studies have shown that the type of filter that removes dissolved salts—the ion exchange filter—can actually be detrimental to the paper because it interferes with hydrogen bonding, thus producing weak sheets. The particulate filter with a carbon cartridge cannot do everything you might want, but it is not detrimental to the paper.

Another way to deal with acids is to neutralize them with a base. Magnesium carbonate and calcium carbonate are the two most commonly used. Magnesium carbonate is more expensive but is better able to bind free iron in water and is more water soluble.

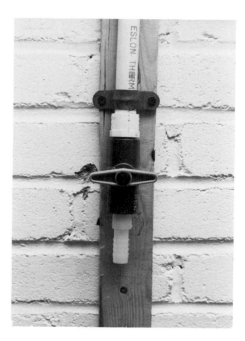

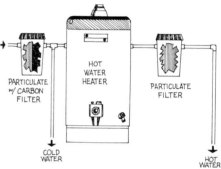

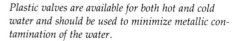

Plastic valves are available for both hot and cold water and should be used to minimize metallic contamination of the water.

In an ideal situation all of the pipes and plumbing fixtures will be plastic. A filter will remove particles, chlorine and fluoride from the cold water line and if hot water is to be used, another particulate filter should be placed after the water heater. This will trap particles picked up in the heater.

Ideally, water used for papermaking will have an abundance of calcium in it and this will compensate for some of the dissolved metals. But if it does not, it should be filtered and/or calcium carbonate should be added until a pH of 7.0 is reached.

Choosing the Fiber

Until the mid-nineteenth century, all fiber for papermaking came from new cloth or rags that were processed at the papermill under carefully controlled conditions to ensure the longevity of the resulting papers. Today papermakers can buy their fibers precooked and partially beaten from some mills. And the available fibers are no longer just cotton and linen rag but include jute, banana fiber (abaca), and over a hundred grades of cotton linter.

Linter is the fiber left on the cotton seed after the long fibers have been removed in the ginning process. This fiber is too short to be spun into cloth but can be used for making paper. It is stiffer and more brittle than the long-fibered cotton, and the paper produced from it is not as strong or supple as that produced from rag. It is a low-shrinkage pulp and can be used in certain types of papers and three-dimensional casting processes.

Commercially produced rag pulp is known as half stuff. It has been prepared in large cookers under extreme pressure and heat and with a high percentage of caustic to reduce the cooking time. It has been partially beaten to the specification of the mill. The resulting pulp has been weakened by this overprocessing. The papermaker loses a great deal of control over results by using this type of pulp, but it has many desirable qualities. It is time saving; it is already cut, cooked, and beaten rag and is available in large quantities at a reasonable cost; it comes in many grades: long-fibered, medium-fibered, muslin, and denim, to mention a few.

The use of synthetics in the textile trade is widespread, and it is often difficult to tell when you have a blended fabric. Because of this, most production papermakers working with cotton use bolts of new cloth or textile cuttings of new cloth. Textile cuttings can be purchased in large quantities from rag sellers who will often guarantee that the entire content of the bale is cotton. Unfortunately, rag merchants usually sell only in large quantities. Used rag can also be purchased from hospitals, laundries, and restaurant linen and towel companies.

There are two simple tests that can be used to determine synthetic fibers. A scrap of synthetic cloth will melt and leave a bead of plastic when burned; cotton or linen will not. In a glass of water, synthetic cloth will float; cotton and linen will absorb water and sink.

Even with these tests it is difficult to determine blended fibers, but in the beater, the synthetics will not fibrillate. The resulting paper will be weak, and as it ages, the synthetic fiber will rapidly deteriorate and turn yellow under mildly acidic conditions, with heat, and in sunlight.

Most preprocessed pulps and cotton linter do not require any additional processing prior to beating. Their pH, however, should be checked.

Although time-consuming in its processing, cloth allows the papermaker the greatest range of potential papers and control over their quality. The cloth can be used uncooked or can be cooked in a mild caustic or by retting. It can be lightly beaten to ensure long fiber length or chopped short. Beginning the papermaking process with a thorough understanding and careful control of the raw materials will help to assure successful results.

Cooking

Cooking is a very important step in preparing the cloth for beating. Although cloth can be used uncooked, cooking will soften and clean the fibers, bleach them, and remove some types of industrial residues such as starch and sizing.

The cloth should first be cut into small squares (one half inch by one half inch). These are placed in a stainless steel or enameled pan (avoid aluminum or cast iron, which will react with the caustic). To this a weak solution of caustic is added. There are several available caustics (see list in chapter 3). Sodium hydroxide, known as caustic soda or supermarket lye, is the most powerful, followed by sodium carbonate, known as soda ash or supermarket washing soda, potassium carbonate, and wood ash.

The concentration of this cooking solution will affect the characteristics of the pulp. The weight of the dry fiber, the weight of the caustic, and the amount of water used are the most important factors in determining the concentration of the cooking solution. A mild solution (based on Oriental proportions for cooking bast fiber) for cotton or linen rag would be 1 kilogram of cloth to 100 grams of caustic in 10 liters of water. This cooking solution could properly be called a 1 percent solution. A 1 percent solution of lye will be more alkaline and cook the fibers in a shorter period of time than a 1 percent solution of washing soda, but the stronger akaline may make the fiber brittle and remove hemicellulose. Slow cooking with a mild caustic is always best for the fiber. **When combining caustic and water, add the dry caustic to the water; never add the water to the dry caustic. The caustic may spit if improperly combined. Eye protection should be worn.**

Once the proportion has been determined and the caustic added to the water, the solution can be brought to a boil and the cloth added and simmered for two hours. Once removed from the heat, the pot of solution and cloth should be allowed to stand until cool, or overnight. The cloth must be thoroughly rinsed in cold running water to remove all residual caustic and to lighten the fiber. If it is completely rinsed, a pH strip placed against the damp fiber will indicate a pH near 7, provided your water supply is near neutral as well.

Once the cloth has been rinsed and tested, it is ready to be broken down into fine fibers for sheet forming.

The Stamper Beater

In both the European and Oriental traditions, machines were developed to eliminate the tedious and time-consuming process of hand beating fiber. The stamper-type beaters were hand-operated or attached to a waterwheel. The cooked material was placed in a basin beneath a heavy wooden or metal shaft to which was attached a foot of hardwood or metal. The shaft was attached to a lifting collar, which raised and then dropped the shaft. The foot beat against the fibers but did not cut them and left the pulp strong and flexible. With its inherent fiber length intact, the beaten pulp produced strong, supple sheets of paper.

The stamper beater was replaced by the Hollander beater, which could process uncooked cloth in a shorter time. But with the special needs of today's hand papermakers and artists, the stamper may once again have useful applications. It is particularly effective on bast fibers, and although it can only process a pound of pulp at one time, that pulp will have unique qualities unattainable by any other beating method. Linen, flax, milkweed, hemp, jute, and the traditional Oriental fibers can be processed. The stamper beater gives additional control to produce the pulp most suitable for the paper needed.

Keeper of the rag cooker, Gandhi Ashram, Ahmedabad, India. Photograph courtesy of Lynn Forgach, Exeter Press, New York.

This pneumatic stamper beater driven by compressed air is suitable for preparing bast fibers. It was built by Lee McDonald Papermaking Supply Company.

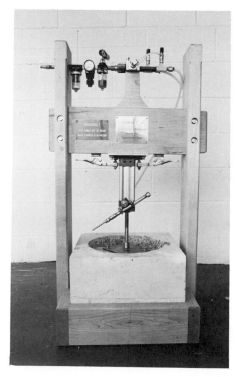

The Hollander Beater

The mechanical and physical characteristics of a Hollander beater determine how well the machine can prepare pulp for a variety of uses and how accurately it can reproduce these results.

Two critical components within the machine are the roller and bedplate. The roller circulates the water in the tub and brings the cloth fragments between it and the bedplate. Here they are cut and separated into individual fibers, which are then fibrillated during the beating process.

The materials used for these two components will affect the resulting paper. The blades of a stainless steel roller and bedplate will develop smooth, rounded edges after repeated use; this reduces the amount of cutting and leaves the fiber longer and well fibrillated. Stainless steel is also noncorrosive and thus maintenance-free. As phosphor bronze or any of the other steel alloys wear down, they develop sharp edges. These edges increase the cutting of the fiber, which is not always desirable. Some may require maintenance if rust develops on them. Aluminum is being used in some of the newer beaters with good results, although there is concern about it reacting with alkaline pulp. Some used laboratory beaters are equipped with lava stone rollers and bedplates. The broad blades of the stones do very little cutting of the cloth and were traditionally used for making glassine. They work well on long fibers, but their porous nature makes them difficult to clean, especially if pigments or fillers are added to the pulp during beating.

Etching of stamper beaters from A Diderot Pictorial Encyclopedia of Trades and Industry.

Based on a historic experimental machine, James Yarnell produces the Oak Park Over-And-Under Umpherston beater. Although its construction is verticle, it has all of the same basic components as the Hollander beater. This small beater holds two gallons of water and one-half pound of pulp. Its heat-treated cast aluminum roller and bedplate, vacuum-formed plastic body, and removable cover make it easy to clean. It is operated by a one-third horsepower motor. With the cover removed, the chassis may be lifted for easy cleaning or making adjustments.

A Hollander beater, with backfall, roller, and bedplate.

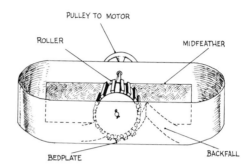

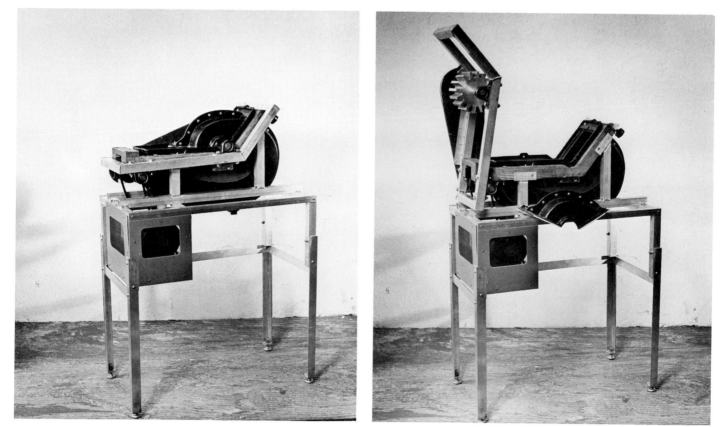

To ensure accuracy during beating and the accurate reproduction of a given pulp, the beater must have a sensitive and calibrated bedplate or roller bar adjustment. The movable member of the two will change from one manufacturer or design to another. On some beaters, the bedplate is mounted on a rubber diaphragm and is raised by a weight or screw system. This diaphragm can be torn under strenuous beating conditions and may need to be replaced occasionally. In other machines the roller bar can be lowered to meet the bedplate. This is a more sensitive type of calibration, allowing for greater distance between the roller and bedplate. With the roller bar raised to its highest position (or the bedplate dropped to its lowest), the pulp circulates freely in the tub. As the space between these two parts is decreased (by raising the bedplate or lowering the roller), the pulp is compressed between them, causing the fibers to rub together and separate. As compression increases, by closing the space, these fibers are further abraded, and fibrillation of their internal and external surfaces occurs. When the roller bar and bedplate are brought together, cutting of the fiber begins.

Often new roller bars have to be "ground in," a process that removes any high spots on the blades and ensures that they are parallel with the bedplate. Carborundum acts as an abrasive. To a one pound beater, a cup of number 80 grade carborundum is added while the machine is operating. The roller and bedplate are slowly brought in contact with each other. This very noisy process ensures even, consistent beating when the high spots have been removed from the roller bars. A permanent magic marker may be used to draw lines along the roller bars before the grinding-in process. High spots and magic marker lines will be ground down at the same time. When all the lines have been removed, the blades of the roller and bedplate will be parallel.

This is the "Corvette Sting Ray" of Hollander beaters. It is manufactured by Twinrocker Equipment, Inc., and features a noncorrosive stainless steel roller and bedplate and a fiberglass body and removable rollguard for easy cleaning. It will pulp all types of cellulose fiber, from rags to straw, and has a capacity of two and one-half pounds of dry material.

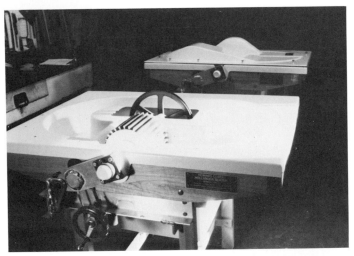

This custom-built, ten-pound beater at the Atelier Royce, a custom paper and collaboration facility in New York City, was designed by Art Schade.

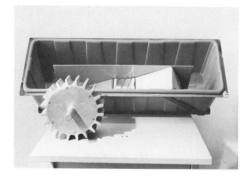

This mock-up shows how a standard off-the-shelf, plastic tub supported by welded angle irons can be modified for an elementary beater. Plans for this are available through Oak Park Press and Papermill.

Roller and bedplate sets may be purchased separately from some manufacturers for those interested in building their own beater. Two of these Oak Park beater rolls can be assembled on one shaft to produce a wide roll for a larger machine.

Behind the roller bar and bedplate is an inclined surface known as the backfall. During the beating process, the pulp is lifted by the roller bar and thrown over this backfall where it slides down the opposite side. This lifting and sliding creates the momentum that keeps the pulp circulating in the tank. The angle of the backfall affects the rate of circulation and the amount of tangling that occurs with certain long-fibered pulps. By reducing the angle, less pulp will accumulate. Most commercially available beaters are intended to be used on wood pulps or other short fibers for which entanglement is not a problem.

The coverguard of the beater fits over the end of the tub containing the roller bar, bedplate, and backfall and controls the amount of splashing that occurs during beating. A removable coverguard greatly aids in the cleaning of the machine between loads. This can be an important consideration when the machine is used for color work or fiber mixing.

The capacity of a beater is determined by the weight of dry fiber to the weight of water. A one and one half pound beater can accommodate one and one half pounds of dry fiber in forty-eight pounds, or six gallons, of water. This concentration will affect the character of the resulting pulp. Higher concentrations—that is, more fiber—will increase the amount of cutting that occurs during beating. Lower concentrations increase the amount of fibrillation that occurs. A well-fibrillated pulp will produce a denser, stronger, more translucent sheet than a pulp whose fibers are overshortened and less fibrillated.

The tub used for beating should be of a noncorrosive material—bronze, painted cast iron, fiberglass, cement, aluminum, or reinforced, sealed wood. It

should be mounted on heavy rubber and on a sturdy table, which may also have rubber under its legs. The beating process is often noisy, so the more cushioning you can provide for the machine, the quieter it will be.

One pound of beaten pulp will produce approximately seventy-five sheets of eight-by-eleven-inch stationery-weight paper. Beaters are available in one-and-one-half, three-, and five-pound sizes, and custom machines can be built for larger loads. Production papermakers may find the one and one half and three-pound machines too small for their needs. Experimental and botanical papermakers may find that these smaller beaters will be adequate for the amount of fiber they can collect and will give them more accurate control over the characteristics of the pulp.

Additives and Coloring Agents

A freshly made sheet of paper, known as waterleaf, is a porous web of cellulose waiting to absorb any liquid applied to it—paint, ink, oily fingerprints. This receptive characteristic of the sheet has caused problems for printers, calligraphers, and artists, and since early times many different materials have been used to counteract this absorbency. Substances have been added to the vat before the sheet is formed or applied to the finished paper, and processes have been developed to rub and polish the surface of the sheets.

Fillers are finely ground, nonfibrous materials, usually minerals, that are added to the pulp near the end of the beating process. They do not penetrate the fiber but coat its surface. Consequently, they make the paper less durable by decreasing its bonding capacity. They settle on and between the fibers, closing the pores of the sheet and producing a smooth surface. They make the paper opaque, heavier, and less absorbent.

Calcium carbonate is an alkaline filler that by repelling water improves printability of the paper for some techniques. It is also an important and inexpensive buffering agent added to counteract acidity. Those who preserve important papers and documents suggest that archival paper should have a residual buffer of between 2 and 3 percent to counteract acids that might come in contact with the sheet during a printing process, through environmental pollution, or in storage with an acid-type paper or mounting board. Three grams of this buffer to every one hundred grams of dry fiber is added to the Hollander beater during the last one-half hour of the beating process. Calcium carbonate in larger percentages is also used to produce high luster on magazine papers and to fill the spaces in thin cigarette papers.

Magnesium carbonate is another and very important alkaline filler used as a buffering agent. It binds free iron molecules better than calcium carbonate. A 3 percent solution of magnesium carbonate is used in the beater. It is more expensive than calcium carbonate but much more effective. Both magnesium carbonate and calcium carbonate will brighten the resulting sheets.

Titanium oxide is highly light-refractive and dramatically increases the brightness of a sheet and coloring agents. It can be used in smaller proportions than other brighteners, consequently weakening the paper less.

Sizings are additives that make the paper less absorbent and easier to write on with a water- or oil-base medium. By encasing the fibers, sizings protect them from oxidation, which causes cellulose decomposition and paper breakdown.

The blades of the Lightnin' mixer sit deep within the barrel. This type of equipment can be used with complete success on commercially processed abaca pulp for sheet forming or on cotton linter pulp for thick, sculptural work. It can also be used to break up linter sheets before further processing in the Hollander beater. It tends to knot cotton pulp and thus is not recommended for preparing cotton for sheet forming.

The Lightnin' mixer is an indispensable aid in preparing certain processed pulp and blending dyes, pigments, retention agents, and sizing.

Sizings differ from fillers in that they also act as adhesives, giving the paper additional strength. There are two types of sizings. Vat or internal sizes are mixed with the pulp in the beater before the sheets are formed. This type is often used on print and watercolor paper. They coat the fibers but leave the structure of the paper quite open, allowing for the absorption of ink and pigment. Surface sizes are applied to dry paper. They coat and seal the surface of the sheet and are often used for calligraphy papers, for which absorption or bleeding of the ink is undesirable.

Starches made from potatoes, corn, rice, and gelatin can be used as vat sizes to give sheets additional strength, stiffness, and a surface sheen. A 5 percent solution acts as a size and an adhesive. The starch must first be soaked in cold water to allow the granules to swell. The solution is then heated slowly until it reaches a temperature of around 75°C (165°F). The quality of the starch will vary depending on how much it is cooked. This solution can be poured into the beater during the last ten minutes of beating to thoroughly mix it with the fiber. It can also be used as a surface size. When gelatin is used, the water must be kept warm to prevent it from setting. Often when a paper is to be surface-sized, it is internally sized first. This gives the sheet more strength during the rewetting process of surface sizing and saves on the amount of surface sizing material used. Sizing solution may be brushed on the dry sheet or may be placed in a tub, and the dry sheets run through this liquid. They may also be soaked for several minutes in the sizing solution. The sheets are then stacked one on top of another and lightly pressed to force the sizing further into the sheets and remove any excess sizing.

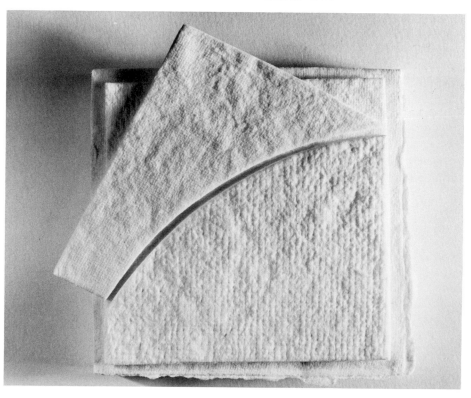

Diagonal Course (detail), Patricia Townsend, 1981. 30″ × 9″.

They are then dried. The pH of starch-sized sheets is neutral, but the gelatin-sized sheet will be slightly acidic (pH 5.5). This may not be detrimental to the sheet, as the gelatin coats and protects the fibers from oxidation.

Waxy, granular Aquapel and liquid Hercon are industrial vat sizings available to the hand papermaker. They are hydrophobic synthetics that coat the fibers but do not change the hardness of the sheet or its color. They appear, through recent tests, to be archivally stable. The proportion of sizing to pulp depends on the type of paper being produced. Eight teaspoons of Hercon may be enough to size seventy-five sheets of paper—or one pound of dry fiber—to be used for stationery, but the nature of the pulp and the desired thickness of the sheets will affect this proportion. Personal experimentation is the best guide. Add the sizing to the pulp in the beater or mixer at the end—in the last two minutes or so—of the beating process. Overmixing will cause the sizing to foam. Mixing in the beater will ensure evenly coated stock.

Another readily available product to be used in the vat as a sizing is methylcellulose, an archival adhesive. It is a dry powder and comes in several grades. It is available in art supply and wallpaper stores. It is resoluble in water, which makes it a reversible sizing. An oversized sheet can be soaked to remove unwanted sizing. It is mixed according to the package directions and then diluted. It can be used as a sizing/adhesive in pulp used for bulky three-dimensional casting projects or can be brushed on flat sheets as a surface sizing. It usually makes the paper stiff. Some grades of methylcellulose will yellow and become brittle with age.

When using fillers, sizings, and adhesives, it is important to remember that a percentage of the liquid will be pressed from the sheets into the felts. Be sure to wash the felts frequently to prevent them from becoming sized as well.

A small percentage, 3 to 5 percent, of an extremely well beaten pulp added to the vat will also improve the smoothness of the surface of a sheet of paper. The fiber length of this pulp should be shortened by overbeating. These fibers will act as fillers between the long fibers and increase the number of hydrogen bonding sites, making the paper stronger.

Alum and rosin are a traditional European duo for sizing. They produce an archivally unstable sheet with a pH of 4.5. They should not be used.

Rabbit skin glue, when soaked and processed like gelatin sizing, can be used as a surface size. The sheets of dry paper can be soaked for up to ten minutes in this warm solution and then pressed and dried. This sizing gives the paper a warm yellow cast and produces a smooth surface on the sheets.

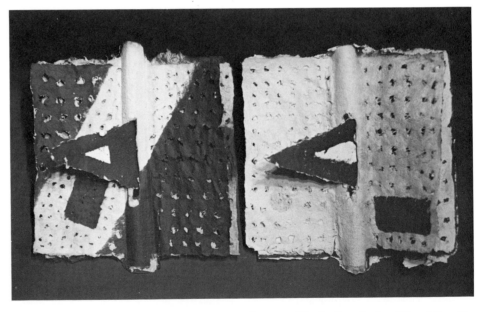

Punctured Book, *Coco Gordon, 22" × 24" × 3". Linen and cotton pulp.*

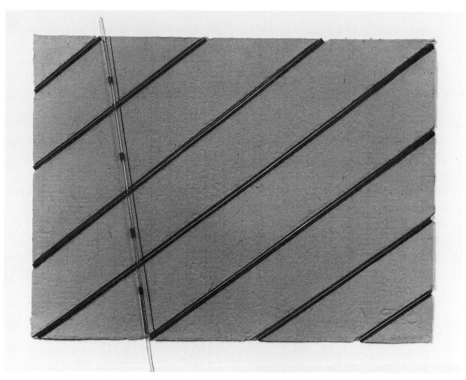

Diagonal Jet Rods, *Judith Sugarman. Handmade paper with grooves formed during sheet forming. Later, acrylic rods were set into these grooves.*

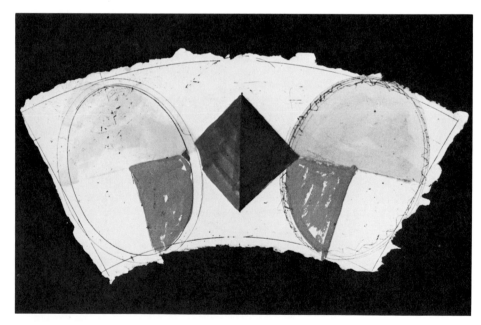

The Mirror Twins, *Sandy Kinnee. Hand-colored intaglio on shaped handmade paper.*

Another type of filler with a different application is the coloring pigments. These are finely ground natural or synthetic particles that impart their characteristic color to the fiber. They have no affinity for cellulose and are insoluble in water. They disperse more evenly throughout the fiber when mixed in the beater. They tend to produce a two-sided color due to their inability to bond to the fiber.

The advantages of pigments as coloring agents are that they are extremely lightfast, produce bright, clean shades of color, and they have a neutral pH.

There are three classes of pigments. The earth pigments or inorganic colorants such as iron oxide, raw sienna, and burnt umber can be used in their original state. Synthetic organic pigments and synthetic inorganic pigments are characterized by a great brilliance, intensity, and range of colors and include cadmiums, chromes, ultramarine blue, and all of the bright colors.

Unfortunately, pigments tend to run or bleed out of wet sheets. This problem can be decreased or eliminated by the use of another group of industrial products called retention agents. Retention agents are binders for internal coloration and affect the electron conditions in the pulp and water solution. They cause the pigment to more permanently bond to the fiber and accordingly reduce bleeding and the tendency of pigments to settle to the bottom side of the sheet. This is most apparent with deeply pigmented pulps. They can be a nuisance, and you have to wash the felts after every use.

Dry pigments should be made into a paste before being added to the pulp. This can be done with a mortar and pestle by adding a few drops of water to the pigment and grinding. Some pigments are very granular and need to be reground while still dry. Others will not immediately mix with water and require the addition of a wetting agent, which penetrates the dry pigment and facilitates dispersion. A few drops of liquid dish soap, denatured alcohol, or methylcellulose can be used for this purpose. It is important to add the wetting agent to the pigment and not vice versa. Once dispersed as a paste, the mixture can be thinned with water and added to the beater for thorough mixing. Small quantities of well-beaten pulp can be mixed with a pigment in the electric kitchen blender as well.

Dyes are another category of coloring agents. They are soluble in water and penetrate the structure of the fiber. They do not require wetting agents during mixing. There are several classes of dyes, some completely inappropriate for use on cellulose fiber.

Direct, fiber reactive, and natural dyes have an affinity for cellulose and will not harm the fiber if properly used. Dyes are less lightfast than pigments but do not interfere with hydrogen bonding or sheet strength. Dyed fiber will leave sheets more flexible and translucent than pigmented pulp and allow the inherent visual qualities of the fiber to show. If properly prepared, separately dyed fibers can be mixed in the vat to produce sheets in which each colored fiber retains its own integrity yet blends to produce a new uniform color, a tweed effect.

Direct dyes have an affinity for cellulose, are easily dissolved in water, and produce strong, bright colors. A brand of direct dyes produced by the Ciba-Geigy company are reputedly more lightfast than most brands. They can be purchased in bulk and are usually mixed in a 2 percent solution (20 grams of dye to 1 liter of water) for medium shades. Table salt is used to mordant the dye and is added at the end of the dyeing procedure and allowed to set for twenty minutes before rinsing.

Fiber-reactive dyes react to and form a chemical bond with cellulose fibers, producing strong, bright colors with a high degree of lightfastness. They are procion dyes and can be purchased in bulk. A 6 percent solution produces medium shades. They require the use of washing soda to set, and thorough rinsing is required to ensure proper removal of this alkaline. They are available in most weaving supply stores and are the dye of choice for most hand papermakers.

Vegetable or natural dyes are considered the most fugitive of the dye types, but many subtle, beautiful colors can come from experimentation with these materials, and they should not be overlooked. There are many good books on natural dyes that can help you in choosing plants. The procedure generally involves macerating the plant material, soaking it overnight, boiling it, straining it, and adding the fiber to the colored liquid. Most recipes mention additional chemical mordants that bond the dye stuff to the fiber. Some of these should be avoided, as the intended fiber for most natural dyes is wool, and these mordants would be detrimental to cellulose. The use of retention agents will help in bonding the dye substance to the fiber. Yellow and red onion skins, walnut shells, madder, logwood, and brazilwood are but a few of the substances that will produce color on papermaking fibers.

Piscine avec trois bleus *(Paper pool #6)*, David Hockney. 72" × 85½". Published by Tyler Graphics Ltd., copyright 1978. This piece was produced as six individual sheets, each measuring 36 inches high by 28½ inches wide, that were butted together to form the total image.

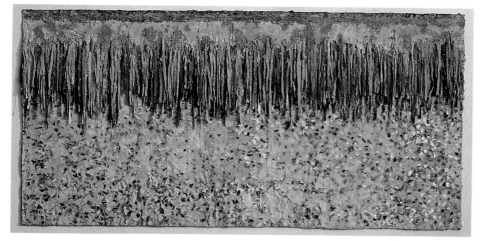

Mosaic, Fredric Amat, 1980. 47" × 94". In this collaborative work produced at Dieu Donne Press and Paper, New York, pulp, textile materials, and paraffin were incorporated with dyes and pigments.

Como, *Gwen Cooper. 24" × 30" × 1". Cast paper with wood.*

Horizontal Stripes (III-19), *Kenneth Noland. 51" × 32". Published by Tyler Graphics Ltd., copyright 1978. The narrow bands are formed on separate sheet molds of the specific shape of the color. Often the artist adds bits of cloth and colored pulp. The final sheet is six layers thick.*

Lomatiums and Iris, *Margaret Ahrens Sahlstrand, 1979. 26" × 37". Cast papers of cotton, day lily, and kozo. In this multiple couched and cast piece, plant parts have been embedded between the layers. Many of the pulps used in Sahlstrand's works are from the same indigenous plants as those embedded between the layers.*

Crazy Bamboo: Yellow Diamond, *Nance O'Banion, 1980. 52" × 52". Abaca fiber, bamboo, and enamel. The large paper for this construction is formed of many small sheets that have been joined at their edges. During the forming process, squares of masking tape were attached to the screen, which formed square openings in the resulting papers.*

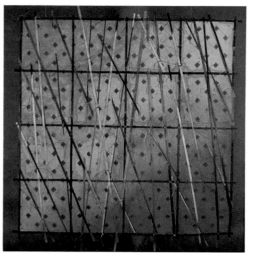

Winter Cycle #3, *Joan Sterrenburg, 1981. 30" × 34". Individual pieces of dyed cotton rag pulp are layered on a structure that supports the work.*

Cochinilla's House, *Fredric Amat, 1980. 88" × 63". Produced in collaboration with Dieu Donne Press and Paper, New York. Cloth, wood, and textural materials are embedded in pulp and later treated with pigments and coloring agents. Photograph by D. James Dee.*

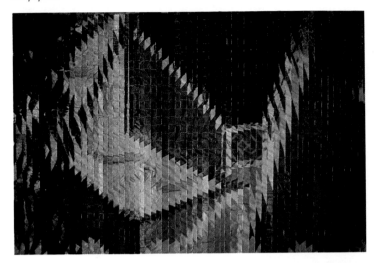

Wall *(detail). The paper strips are held together by warp threads. These widely spaced threads give the form its structure but do not hide the quality of the papers.*

Wall, *Katarina Weslien, 1980. 65″ × 31″. This enormous piece incorporates machinemade and handmade paper that has been laminated and used as a weft material.*

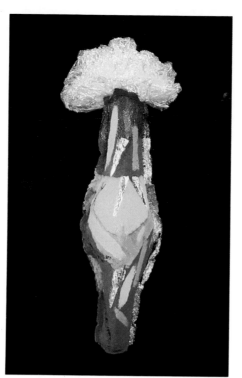

Splat III, *Robert Arneson, 1981. 43″ × 42″ × 13″. Cast and hand-worked pulp with pigments. Published by the Experimental Printmaking Studio.*

Lagniappe II, *Lynda Benglis, 1979. 38″ × 13″ × 8″. Cast pigmented paper, glitter, gold leaf, and polypropylene. Produced at Exeter Press, New York.*

Bangalore, *Terrance La Noue. 34″ × 43″ × ½″. Produced at Exeter Press. Photograph courtesy of 724 Prints, New York.*

Rhythm #2, *Tova Beck Friedman, 1981. 36" × 26". This work was produced in sections, each of a different fiber and color. The sections and cloth fragments were then assembled. The pulps used were abaca, hand-processed banana fiber, and cotton cloth. Photograph by D. James Dee.*

Untitled, *Deborah Bryant, 1981. 33" × 42". Hand-formed pigmented paper.*

Structural Metaphor, *Nance O'Banion, 1981. 6' × 10'. Abaca and paint. The smaller dash marks are openings in the sheets formed with tape during sheet forming. The work is displayed in two pieces so that people can walk between the sections.*

Configuration, *Mildred Fischer, 1978. 13″ ×
13″. Linen pulp with prewoven linen elements and
silk threads.*

Fragments From Our Past, *Lilian Bell, 1978.
18″ × 16″. Redwood, Manila hemp, and mulberry
fibers. Skilled in Oriental paper techniques, the artist embedded other papers, cloth, and objects between thin layers of translucent pulps, which
reveal ghostlike images of the objects.*

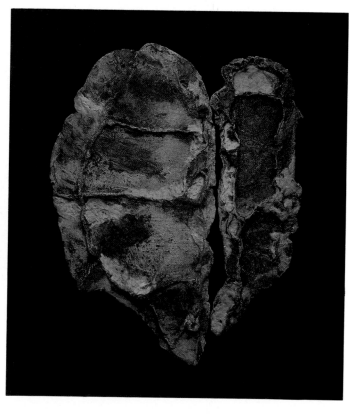

Untitled, *Constance Miller, 1981. 12″ × 16″.
This many-layered piece is made of dyed pulps, textile materials, and reeds.*

Broken Circle, *Golda Lewis, 1981. 18½″ ×
14½″. Terra cotta and paper. The artist applied
pulp and stain to the surface of cast terra cotta.*

Rampant Zebra Runner, *Lin Fife, 1981. 3' × 7'. Dyed, hand-formed paper.*

NAHANY, *Barbara Schwartz, 1981. 85" × 56" × 18". Casein on handmade paper over wire lath. Photograph by Pelka/Noble and courtesy of Willard Gallery, New York.*

Untitled, *Eve Eisenstadt. 9' × 11'. This work was constructed in triangular modular units at the Twinrocker Paper Company. It and others of this series are displayed using Velcro tape, a two-sided textile fastener. This allows for quick and easy installation in a variety of arrangements.*

Extensive research in the use of color and retention agents has been done by artist/papermaker Elaine Koretsky. She suggests mixing 15 milliliters of liquid retention agent with one-half liter of water, letting this set for ten minutes, adding it to each pound of pulp at the end of the dyeing process, and mixing the water, retention agent, and pulp together for ten minutes. The pulp should be tested for bleeding by straining it through a sieve or colander. If it still bleeds, more retention agent should be added in increments of 5 milliliters mixed in one-half liter of water. The pulp and retention agent should be mixed again for ten minutes. With some dyes, especially natural dyes, better retention is achieved if the pulp and dye mixture is allowed to set overnight. Even then, some will bleed. In all cases, a thorough rinsing after dyeing is needed to remove excess dye, retention agent, and salt from the pulp before it is used in sheet forming.

By taping colored papers in a sunny window and placing them near fluorescent and incandescent light bulbs, some relative tests can be made for lightfastness. An additional piece of the colored paper should be stored in a dark place for comparison after one week, two weeks, and one month under the three light conditions. Lightfastness is important for color that will be used in artworks and book covers and less important for temporary papers such as stationery.

A word of warning about dyes and pigments. Dust from these can enter the bloodstream directly through the lungs. This is a very great danger. A face mask should *always* be worn when working with these compounds. Also, dyeing should never be done in the kitchen where utensils or food may be contaminated. Rubber gloves should also be worn to prevent skin irritations. Dye chemicals may cause cancer, so use all precautions when working with them.

The following color chart suggests pigments that are easily mixed with pulps. The use of a retention agent, methylcellulose, or sizing improves the binding of the pigment to the fibers. These pigments were tested on pulp well hydrated in a Hollander beater and pigmented by hand mixing. This research was done at Dieu Donne Press and Paper in New York City, using Fezandie and Sperrle dry artist pigments.

Red	Yellow	Orange	Green
Ruby	Cobalt	Cadmium extra deep	Ultramarine
Cadmium deep	Mars	Cadmium medium	Chrome oxide opaque
Cadmium light	Titian	Cadmium deep	Viridian
Vermilion light	French ochre medium	Orange mineral	Cobalt light
Cardinal	French ochre deep		Cobalt deep
Mars red	Golden	**Brown**	
Vermilion deep	Barium chromate	Burnt umber	**Blue**
Garnet	Cadmium deep	Mars brown	Cerulean
Pozzuoli	Cadmium medium	Burnt sienna	Manganese
Venetian	Golden ochre		Turquoise
Burgundy		**Black**	
Terra rosa		Mars	**Violet**
Indian		Ivory	Manganese
			Mars violet
			Violet ochre "B"
			Ultramarine
			Cobalt

The Mold

European-style sheet forming requires the lifting and holding of large quantities of pulp and water. Consequently, the mold for this technique must be substantial. Traditionally, the mold consisted of a frame and deckle of mahogany and white pine ribs. Both woods are water-resistant, strong, and lightweight. The function of the ribs is to keep the surface of the mold flat during sheet forming. This allows even distribution of pulp and a resulting uniformly thick sheet. The ribs also give the papermaker a surface to press against during the couching procedure. The rib system is covered with two layers of wire mesh. A coarser layer is sewn directly to the ribs and provides a separation between them and the final surface on which the sheets are formed. Without this underlayer, water passing through the mesh will hit the ribs and cause the fibers in the sheet to separate enough to make a slight shadow or watermark in the paper. The deckle, which rests on top of the mold, restrains the pulp and determines the shape and thickness of the sheet by its own shape and thickness. In a production mill there is one deckle for every two molds so that the pulp on one can drain while the next is being used for forming. Often these deckles are divided so that more than one sheet of paper can be formed at a time.

To construct your own mold, the mahogany stock for the frame should be 1½ inches deep and ½ inch thick, joined at the corners with dovetail joints and water-resistant glue. The pine ribs should be 1 inch deep and ¼ inch thick, tapered to a thin edge. Doweled ends should protrude on either end of the wider side of the ribs. These ends should be less than ½ inch long, as they will be

A European mold and deckle.

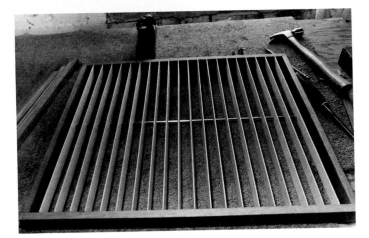

A metal rod is placed through holes in the center of each rib on this large mold for extra reinforcement. Cross bracing may also be necessary on very large molds.

mounted without glue in the sides of the mold in holes set 1 to 1¼ inches apart (a slightly wider spacing of 1¼ inches makes the sewing of the wire surface easier). The tapered edges of the ribs should extend slightly above the surface of the frame to be sanded down later to give the mold a slightly raised center, or crown, which will aid in couching the sheets. The ribs are also pierced with holes every ½ inch along their length and in the center of their width. Through these, the layers of wire mesh will be sewn with a fine wire, a mono-filament fishing line, or a sturdy poly-ester thread. (The consideration here is that the thread should not rot or stretch after frequent exposure to water.)

The layers of mesh can be brass, phos-phor bronze, or plastic. The underlayer is coarse, with a gauge of four to eight wires to the inch in each direction, and is sewn to the ribs. The top layer can be woven wire or plastic or a series of wire rods twined together. A fine woven screen of forty to sixty mesh will pro-duce a textureless surface on the sheet. A twined wire surface known as laid-line, with seventeen to twenty-one wires to the inch, will produce a more textured sheet that contains an image of the wires when held up to a light. With both lay-ers sewn in place, thin brass strips are tacked down over the ends of the wire mesh to protect and prevent the accumu-lation of pulp along these edges. All metal used in the construction of molds must be noncorrosive brass, copper, stainless steel, or aluminum.

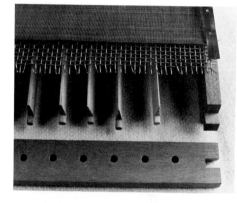

The doweled tapered ribs fit unglued into the long side of the mold. To these are sewn a heavy gauge underwire and a fine gauge top wire, the edges of which are secured with brass strips. Dovetail joints join the corners of the frame, and a water-resistant glue is applied to these joints. A hole is drilled from the top to the bottom at the corners, and a dowel is hammered in place to further secure them.

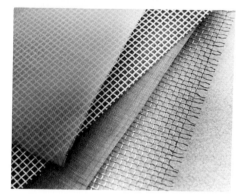

Lightweight plastic screens (the two on the left) can be used in place of the traditional phosphor bronze screens (on the right).

A laid-line screen can be made from lightweight Monel (metal fishing wire) and .035 gauge or finer stainless steel or bronze rods, available at welding supply stores. The wire is twisted around the rods, holding them in place. This method can produce a screen of fourteen to sixteen rods to the inch.

Across the top width of a working surface (as wide as the rods are long) hammer nails every one and one quarter inches. Leave some of the nail protruding.

For each nail, cut a piece of wire seven times the intended length of the final mold surface. Wrap a spool onto each end of each wire, nearly to the middle of the wire. Use a rubber band to hold the wire on the spools. Bend the middle of each wire in half around a nail. Twist each wire several times before inserting the first rod.

Place a rod between the wires and twist the wires once. Repeat this process across the length of the rod until all the spools have been twisted. This locks the rod in place. Place the next rod between the wires and repeat the process. Continue with the remaining rods.

The mahogany stock for the deckle should be 1½ inches wide and 1¾ inches thick. It is shaped to fit over the top and part of the way down the side of the frame. Because of the eventual expansion and contraction of the frame when wet, the deckle should fit loosely when made. The corners can be joined in a number of ways, but strength and inflexibility should be the main concerns. The wood pieces that make up the width of the deckle, those not held by the papermaker's hands, are wedge-shaped, with the thinner edge toward the inside. The wedge allows the wave of excess water and pulp to move freely off of the mold surface during sheet forming. The wood in most traditional molds was left

untreated, but a penetrating oil (Thompson's Water Sealer) can be used and reapplied yearly. Molds and deckles are always stored by tying them together as a unit to prevent warping. The unit is stored flat with the mold resting on its deckle.

The size of a mold depends on the need of the paper. Emperor was the name given to a paper 48 by 72 inches, the largest handmade paper ever produced in Europe. Antiquarian, a 31-by-53-inch paper produced by the James Whatman Company in England, was used for drawing and printing large books and maps. Elephant, 23 by 28 inches, was a drawing and printing paper. There was also Double Elephant, 26¾ by 40 inches. Foolscap, 13½ by 17 inches, was a printing and writing paper with the impression of a court jester in its surface. Demy was a standard printing paper measuring 17½ by 22½ inches, and Billet Note, at 6 by 8 inches, was an old-style size for stationery.

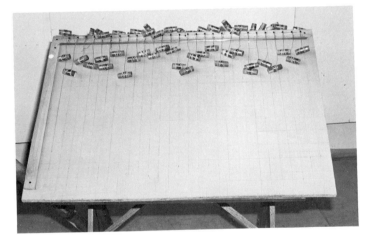

Drawn lines on the working surface make it easier to keep the wires straight as you work. As the work proceeds, flat sticks nailed to the working surface will hold the laid-line surface in place.

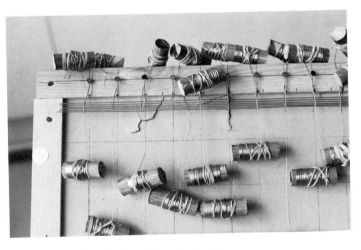

Spools can be made of dowels and the wire is held in place with rubber bands.

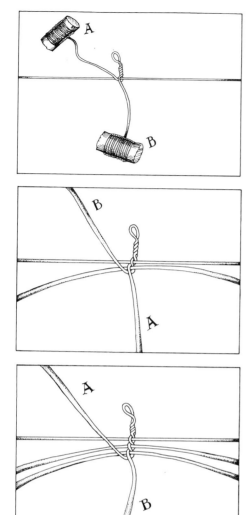

A single twist holds the wires in place.

These production molds were used for making watermarked stationery and envelopes. Courtesy of the Crane Paper Museum.

Watermarks

A watermark is a design attached to or impressed in the surface of a rigid metal mold and first appeared in European paper toward the end of the thirteenth century in Italy. The image appears when the sheet is held up to a light and will be either lighter than the base sheet, if the mark is sewn *onto* the screen, or darker than the base paper, if the image is formed *in* the screen. The material used to make the image affects the distribution of pulp on the mold during the sheet-forming process.

There are many possible reasons for the invention of watermarks. It could have been, as it is today, to identify and advertise the manufacturer of the paper. These symbols may have been used to identify the size or quality of the sheets, or they may have been more mystical, identifying secret brotherhoods or religious beliefs. A more practical explanation may be that they served as a simple way to identify pairs of molds, since in production mills two molds and one deckle are used for each size of paper being made.

In any case, a watermark is still an enchanting and magical image, a creative step in the sheet of paper, only to be fully appreciated when held up to a light.

The success of a watermark is based on the kind of pulp used and the weight of the resulting paper. A short-fibered pulp works best because its fibers settle into the fine detail of the image. This image will appear clearest in thin stationery-weight paper. Due to the shortness of the fibers and the thinness of the sheets, it is important that the pulp be well fibrillated to give strength and density to the paper. A lightly beaten pulp would produce a more opaque, bulky sheet, obscuring detail in the image.

This raised watermark is soldered directly to the woven screen.

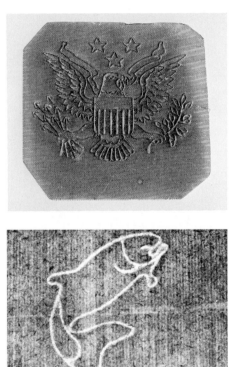

These images were created by raised wire. The lower right one shows a papermaker at a traditional screw press. A simple, temporary watermark can be made by sewing pieces of a coat hanger to a screen. A square wire could be used to make a crisper image.

Another casting is made of the plaster mold. This will serve as the die or surface on which the mold screen will be shaped. This casting is made of a metal-filled epoxy called Devcon B. (3)

This completed shadow mark was made by Mike Dorsa of the Terrapin Paper Mill, Cincinnati, Ohio. It is part of the title page of Images of the Vent Museum, *a portfolio of photographic images of ventriloquial dolls in the collection of the Vent Haven Museum. A light source behind the sheet reveals the image.*

This image was carved into a ¾-inch-thick block of wax on a light table. The key to making this type of mark is the carving process. A two-dimensional image is carved into a relief, and the image will appear again as a two-dimensional watermark. (1)

The wax is covered with a thin layer of petroleum jelly, and a plaster mold is made of this surface. The petroleum jelly aids in releasing the wax from the plaster after the plaster has hardened. (2)

Number 60 mesh stainless steel screen is then placed between the plaster and Devcon molds and pressed in the hydraulic press to emboss the wire. This wire surface is then attached to a European-style mold for sheet forming. The pulp used should be very short-fibered cotton linter. (4)

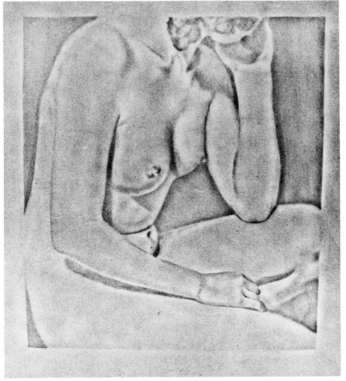

Other examples of shadow marks from the collection of the Dard Hunter Paper Museum shown with a light source behind them.

Felts

Felts for papermaking are an important and expensive part of the process. The newly formed sheets are couched onto them, and they impart a texture to the paper's surface. During pressing, they act as spacers, allowing for the rapid removal of water from the post.

Felts can be made of any material, but traditionally they are wool and are woven. They are available new and used through large papermills and come treated and untreated. The treatment is to prevent mildew and bacterial damage and reduces shrinkage of the felt. Most large mills now use synthetic blends, which are not as absorbent but are readily available.

There are two types of wool felts, woven and needled. Both will affect the surface finish of the final sheet. Needled felts have a woven structure through which wool fibers have been driven back and forth to create a nap. This nap hides the structure of the weaving and produces paper with a very smooth surface. Woven felts lack this nap and produce paper with more texture or tooth.

Used felts from the paper industry often are available free. They usually contain large amounts of sizing or filler materials and need to be washed thoroughly before using.

Felts are woven on a loom. The loom has a series of threads, called the warp, that can be of infinite length and are held under tension during the weaving process. The threads that cross the width of the loom and that are woven between the warp threads are called the weft. These threads are not under tension. Before cutting a large piece of wool felt into usable pieces it is important to determine which direction the warp and weft are lying. Wool felts can shrink 15 percent in the direction of the warp and increase 15 percent in the direction of the weft upon washing. When cutting felts, it is important to remember this.

Determining the warp and weft can be difficult. If you are buying a whole felt from industry, it will be easy because the felt will be many times longer than it is wide, and the warp is always the longest measurement. If you are buying a large piece of cut felt, check the edges for selvage, which is a clean, smooth edge produced during the weaving process as the weft threads return across the warp threads. The selvage will run in the direction of the warp threads. When possible, try to cut the felts 4 inches larger in each direction than the actual size of your paper. For example, a felt for a 9 by 12 inch mold should be cut 13 by 16 inches. This extra material will extract more water from your sheets and make couching easier.

Aside from true papermaker's felts, many other materials can be used: old wool blankets, woolen yard goods, cotton cloth, bedsheets, and some nonwoven textile materials. These can also be used in conjunction with true felts to produce other textures on the final sheet of paper.

All felts need constant attention when they are wet. Mildew will appear as dark spots on the felt, and bacteria can cause holes and disintegration of the fiber.

The easiest way to eliminate these problems is to wash the felts frequently in mild dish soap and ammonia and to keep them dry when not in use. Hanging them in sunlight will destroy bacterial growth and moth eggs. Dry felts should also be stored in plastic bags with a few mothballs to prevent moth infestation.

Often wool felts will become stained with dyes and pigments. Do not try to remove these with chlorine bleach. It will make the wool dry and brittle, discolor it, and reduce the life of the felt. The best solution is to have two sets of felts, one for white and one for color work.

Traditional papermakers' felts are 100 percent wool and are extremely absorbent. An assortment of other materials can be used to create different textures on the finished paper.

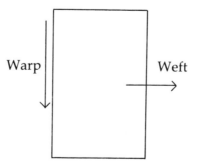

Warp Weft

The Press

Pressing serves two functions. First, it removes water from the felt and pulp, changing the wet pulp into paper. This speeds the drying process and begins hydrogen bonding. This initial pressure decreases the bulk and opacity of the sheet by forcing the flexible fibers into intimate contact with each other where they will eventually bond. Second, pressing affects the surface of the final sheet. This is determined also by your choice of felts. Additionally, a press can be used as a restraining device to keep paper flat while it dries. For this purpose alone, it is very helpful to have a second press in the mill.

Presses can be manual or hydraulic, purchased or homemade. One small mill I visited pressed the papers by placing a board over them and a sewing machine and small appliances on top of the board. Artists have been known to park their cars on plywood board laid over large paper pieces. The press should suit the project. For production papermaking, it should be dependable, easy to use, and powerful enough to extract large amounts of water.

The frame for a press can be built of welded steel or structural aluminum I beams. The pressbed and the platens should be level, smooth, and parallel to each other. This will help ensure even pressing. They should be surfaced with marine plywood and sealed to prevent moisture absorption. Hydraulic car jacks can be used to exert pressure. Their effectiveness can be increased by lengthening the steel bar used to operate them. All metal parts should be painted with an epoxy or marine paint to prevent rust.

A traditional post consisted of 6 quires of paper with a felt between each sheet. A quire consisted of 24 sheets. All 144 sheets and felts were pressed at one time. A post this large is prone to distortion during pressing; the middle sheets stretch and become larger. It is difficult to couch on such a pile because the center is crowned due to the thickness of the wet papers below. Contemporary papermakers deal with this problem in several ways. The easiest solution is to form smaller posts, usually of 50 sheets. Strips of cut felt can be placed in the post along the edges of the paper, or the felts can be rolled back. These additional felts act as spacers and keep the post level, making couching easier.

The first pressing of the post should be hard and fast. Its function is to remove as much water as possible and leave the sheets manageable for further processing. This pressing should only take three or four minutes. After the post is removed from the press, the papers can be lifted from the felts—they are strong enough to hold together with only minimal if any distortion—then transferred to another set of dry felts, and placed back in the press for a long, slow pressing. At this stage, they could be left in the press overnight. When removed from the second set of felts, they will bear the texture of the felts and can be dried or repressed to smooth their surface. In the next pressing, the twice pressed papers are piled directly on top of one another on a single felt and pressed with less pressure. They might bond together if too much pressure is applied. This feltless pressing can be done many times to smooth the surface further; each time, the sheets should be separated and restacked. This paper-to-paper pressing is called cold pressing. After the surface is sufficiently smooth, the sheets can be dried or pressed again between polished metal plates to create an exceptionally smooth, calendered surface. This procedure, though it doesn't involve high temperatures, is known as hot pressing.

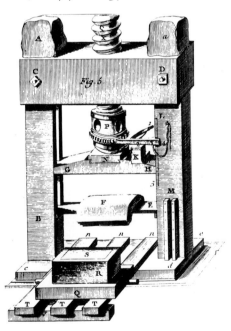

A traditional papermaking press.

With the addition of wooden boards to extend the pressing surface, this traditional screw book press is used at the Carriage House Hand Paper Works in Brookline, Massachusetts.

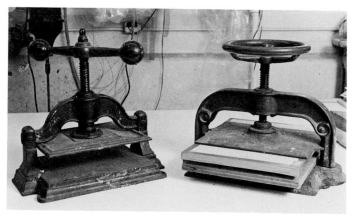

Book binding presses can be used to press small sheets.

This all-aluminum hydraulic jack press was designed especially for hand papermaking by Twinrocker Equipment, Inc. The bedplates are laminated plywood coated with polyurethane. Springs mounted on either side of the press return the platens to their original position after pressing. The press is mounted on casters for easy repositioning in the mill.

The "Ibis" press has a movable bed that adjusts to the height of any work table for easy maneuvering of heavy posts of paper. It is manufactured by Ibis Paper Works and Armadillo Ironworks. Photograph by Jeff Warner.

A Book of Hands, *Bilgé Friedlaender, 1978. 10"*
× 10". Bamboo, cloth, and paper.

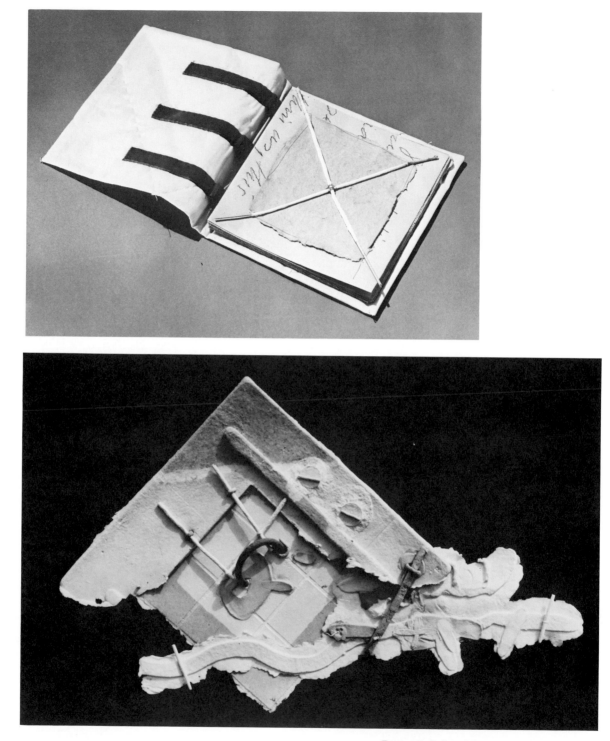

Reston Relief, *Ted Ramsey, 1980. 35" long. Cotton rag.*

Irradiated Fragment, *Golda Lewis, 1980. 19½"
× 16". Terra cotta and paper.*

Jacobras, *Barbara Schwartz, 1980. 80" × 32" ×
7". Casein on handmade paper over wire mesh.*

4-49

Untitled, *Susan Lyman, 1982. 75″ × 70″ × 55″.*
Reed, bamboo, Nepalese paper, paint.

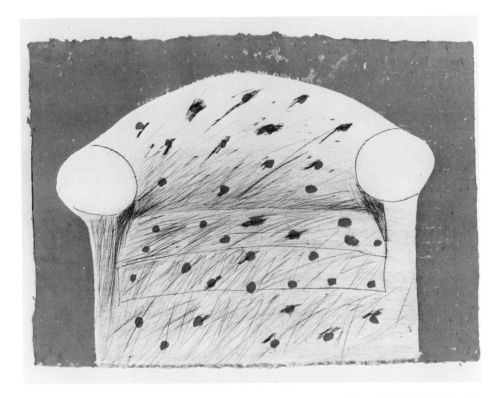

Camelback, *Kingsley Parker, 1982. 22″ × 30″. Edition of 20. Multiple couched image with drypoint etching. Photograph by D. James Dee.*

Big Red, *Beverly Plummer, 1981. 26″ × 23″. Cotton, mulberry, and kudzu fiber with procion dye.*

Proportion Falls Away, *Kathryn Clark, 1981.
34" × 48". Handmade paper, color laminations,
embedments, and collage.*

Fleur Du Mal, *Paul Wong, 1980. Pigmented linen and cotton rag.*

Drying

The key to successful drying is the slow, controlled removal of water. As the fibers dry, they shrink laterally, and this shrinkage can produce warping and cockling in the paper. There are several ways to control this shrinkage. By placing ten to fifteen sheets of damp paper on top of one another and pressing them together, they will temporarily bond and form a thick unit that can be left to air dry in a cool place. The thickness of this packet of sheets will help minimize the distortion of each individual sheet. Because they are not being held flat during their drying, the fibers will be able to shrink to a greater degree, producing a paper with great dimensional stability and strength. Upon drying, these papers can be easily separated and lightly re-pressed to remove any distortions caused during their parting. In spite of producing a superior paper, this system has several drawbacks. It may take a week or longer for the paper to dry, and this requires the continuous availability of a rack in a temperature- and humidity-controlled room. The surface of the sheet will be less smooth than that produced by some other methods.

Twice pressed, damp sheets can be placed between folded blotters and dried through a series of exchanges. The blotters should be approximately the same size as the paper. The area of the blotter larger than the paper will distort after several usings, so blotters should be cut for each size paper being produced. A pile of paper and blotters should be weighted by some means or can be left in the press overnight. The blotters should be changed several times a day until the sheets are dry; both will not feel cold at this point. A test can be made by removing one sheet and observing it. If it begins to distort, the paper is not dry. Once you feel the sheets are dry, they can be placed together and allowed to age. During this aging period, the dry sheets become accustomed to the humidity of the atmosphere, and the sizing matures.

There are several variations of the blotter exchange method that can be used to speed the process. Homosote, a wall-board available at lumberyards, can be cut to the size of the blotters and painted with a white latex paint. These boards will absorb water and can be placed between the blotters to speed the capillary removal of water from the pile. They, as well as the blotters, need to be dried between pressings to prevent the formation of mildew.

Another method uses corrugated card-board with A flute corrugations. Cut the cardboard to the size of the homosote. The grooves in the cardboard should run the length of the homosote. The cardboard should be placed between every two homosote boards in the pile, and because it is acidic, should not be placed in contact with the damp blotter. The layers of cardboard act as absorbent spacers, allowing air to pass through the pile of drying papers. By placing a fan in front of this pile, papers can be dried quickly, often without ever changing the blotters. The fan can be accompanied by an electric heater, but moving air alone works very well and costs less.

Drum dryers, used in photography studios, can also be used to dry papers. They consist of a heated stainless steel drum and cloth cover that holds the sheet against it. They dry the paper quickly, but the sheets often retain the slight curve of the drum.

Post and Paper 81-17, *Ann Flaten Pixley, 1981.*
45' × 14' × 5".

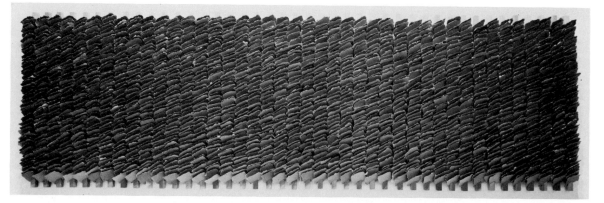

Building a Small Papermill

The size of the mill depends on the work that will be done there. Using an electric blender and simple equipment, a kitchen may be large enough. If you decide to build a more elaborate facility, here are a few things to consider.

A floor drain eliminates endless mopping of water. If you can find a room with a drain, papermaking will be easier. Painting the floor with a nonskid paint will reduce slipping. You will also need a good source of water (filtered) and natural light. It is very difficult to judge color under artificial conditions. It is also hard to spend long hours under fluorescent lighting. The size of the room is important, and you can never have enough space. A large basement or garage can be used. You will also want an extra room for storing dry pulps, papers, pigments, felts, and plaster. You may also want to build an enclosure for your beater to soundproof it. The interior of this enclosure should be painted with enamel or covered with Formica or tile. Water will splash everywhere when you are cleaning the beater. This enclosure should be on the floor with a drain. Mounting the beater and the table on heavy rubber will help reduce vibration and sound.

The table on which the felts are placed during couching should be the same height as the bottom platen of your press. This will allow you to push the post of wet felts and paper into the press without lifting it.

If possible, mount everything on wheels. This will eliminate needless lifting and will make your studio space more flexible. The buckets in which you store your pulp should be of heavy gauge plastic set on a platform with wheels. Portable plastic sinks and tables with folding saw horse-type legs come in handy and make the space more flexible.

Seal everything. Coat all of the wood in the mill with polyurethane or enamel paint. Use only plastic or noncorroding materials for buckets, sieves, strainers, scissors, and even screws during construction. Water goes everywhere in a papermill. Anticipate this.

Vats can be made of marine plywood covered with fiberglass. Prefabricated fiberglass tubs used for outdoor lily ponds work well and are available at greenhouses. They come in a range of sizes and shapes and are lightweight. A simple frame of boards, for example, one inch by ten inches, or cut plywood set on the floor and lined with sheet plastic, can be used as a temporary vat for large projects and can be dismantled easily when the project is over.

If cloth for pulp is purchased by the bolt, it can be taken to a seam binding company where, for a fee, it can be cut into rolls of any width. These strips of fabric can then be cut into smaller pieces with an electric pattern cutter, a cutting machine used in the clothing industry to cut through many layers of cloth. It can be mounted upside down on a table, and the cloth strips, or cloth in any form, can be fed between its rotating blades.

Drying boards for Oriental-style sheet drying can be made of plywood covered with tile board, an inexpensive Formicalike surface. Panel adhesive, available at lumberyards, can be used to adhere the tile board to both sides of the plywood. Frames for European air drying can be covered with fiberglass window screen. These frames can be supported in a rack and can be slid like drawers for easy placement of the paper.

The frames can be made of plastic diffusion grating used to cover fluorescent light fixtures. These can then be covered with fiberglass screening and can serve many drying purposes in the mill. When removed from the rack, they can be used to dry plaster molds or large amounts of pulp or vegetable matter.

Two scales are needed in most mills, one to weigh pounds of dry fiber and one to weigh grams of pigment. A ceramic mortar and pestle, dust mask, and accurate liquid measuring containers are also needed. A hot plate in the mill for cooking fibers is also suggested. A small scrub brush will help remove pulp from your felts after sheet forming, and a pair of tweezers will help remove unwanted hairs or contamination from the sheet on your mold during sheet forming. Rubber boots and aprons will help to keep you dry through it all.

A heavy-duty washing machine is essential for keeping your felts in good condition, and many clotheslines are needed for drying felts and blotters. The closer your mill is to the washer, the less lifting you will have to do. Electric fans will help dry everything, from felts to papers, even the floor.

A table covered with frosted glass and lit from beneath with a fluorescent light is helpful when examining papers for flaws. This caretaking is important for establishing quality.

Setting up a small mill can be a very costly venture and is one to consider carefully. Your local papermaker can be very helpful with these matters. It is very important to set up a good bookkeeping system at the beginning. A great deal of tax money can be saved if you keep accurate records. Most state or city arts organizations have accountants and lawyers to help you with these matters. Don't hesitate to use them.

The layout of the mill is very important to daily operations. The water should be filtered (**1**), and the outlets should be located at spots throughout the mill where the water will be needed. To eliminate transporting quantities of pulp and water around the room, arrange the equipment in the order of the process. The Hollander beater (**2**) and Lightnin' mixer (**3**) should be near the vat (**4**). The couching table (**5**) should roll to the press (**6**), and the drying boards (**7**) and drying rack (**8**) should be close at hand. Extra tables (**9**) for working with the dry paper should be near the drying area, and extra room should be available for additional temporary equipment such as a vacuum table (**10**). The whole procedure can be simplified if the room has a floor drain (**11**). A flat shelf is essential for storing the molds to prevent them from warping (**12**).

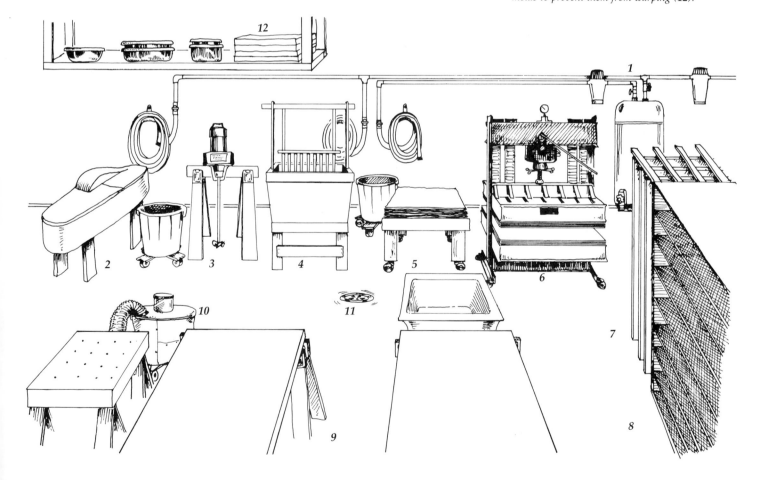

Multiple Sheet Forming

Deckles can be made to produce more than one sheet of paper at a time on the mold.

1

The deckle is removed. . .

3

2

With the deckle in place, the mold is dipped into the vat.

5

The mold is pressed on the felt.

Revealing four separate sheets.

4

6
The sheets remain attached to the cloth. Another felt is placed on top of the freshly formed sheets and the process is repeated.

7
The pile of felts and papers are put in the press and the excess water is removed.

5 | *Contemporary Sculptural Techniques*

Loop, Cynthia Carlson. 25" × 27" × 4". Cast paper produced at Exeter Press. Photograph courtesy of 724 Prints, New York.

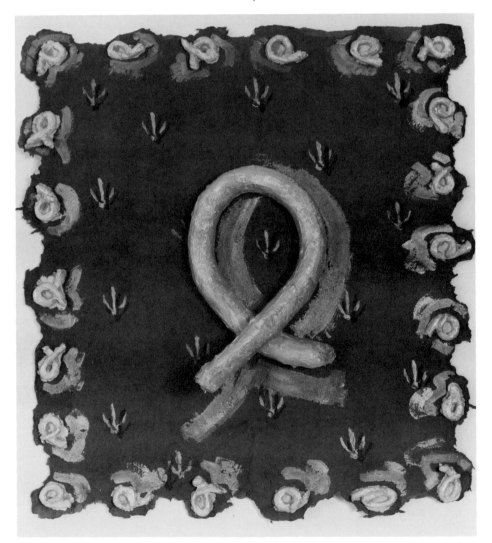

Traditional papermaking is a form of casting. The flat, rectangular shapes formed on the mold are usually bound in books or covered with an image. But the papermaker's craft and materials offer today's artists fertile ground for experimentation. Each pulp has its own inherent texture, color, and transparency, which can be used as is or pigmented or dyed. Sizing and adhesives can be added to change further its character. Its malleable nature makes it a much sought-after material.

With some water removed, pulp can be manipulated by hand much like clay. Found objects can act as armatures to support the image or can be added for texture. The wet pulp can be formed in and easily removed from conventional plaster or rubber molds. It can be sprayed from modified air guns, and shaped molds can be dipped into a vat of pulp to form thin translucent, three-dimensional objects.

Many artists have invented new methods and equipment for working with the materials to express their ideas. These inventions and the contemporary paper art object itself will undoubtedly stand as our contribution to paper's ever-expanding history.

Hand Manipulation

Hand manipulation is simple, inexpensive, and quick in comparison with more traditional papermaking techniques. It can be used to create large forms or sheets, since traditional molds are not required. A beaten pulp can be strained to remove excess water and handled much as clay is handled. It can be pushed into forms or around them. Different colored pulps can be laid next to each other to create imagery viewable from both the front and the back. If viewing from only one side is intended, additional layers of pulp can be used to enclose an armature or hanging device or to create additional thickness and bulk.

Lin Fife applies colored pulp to areas of the drawn image of her piece Interrupted Carpet. *(See finished work in color section.)*

The fibers in this procedure do not interweave as they would in a traditional, vat-formed sheet. Although the sheer bulk of the work may hold it together, binders (methylcellulose or other high-grade archival adhesives) are generally added to the wet pulp to give the work added or necessary strength. On some thin pieces, the back of the work can be coated with gesso for additional strength.

The drying time for thick pieces can be reduced by pressing them with sponges to remove excess water. Felt can be pressed on flat pieces to smooth the surface. If the work is flat but too large for a conventional press, improvised presses can be made using building blocks as weights. A fan and heat lamp will speed drying.

As this kind of work dries, it may become distorted, but this effect can be minimized by using a low-shrinkage pulp such as cotton linter or abaca or by adding a filler such as clay. The work should be dried slowly and evenly and may be weighted in areas as it dries.

When working in such a free method, certain precautions need to be taken. As the water evaporates from the work, any dissolved materials in the pulp will be carried with it and deposited on the high spots of the casting. This contamination appears as brown stains. It can be eliminated by filtering the water system. If the water is filtered and stains still appear, the contamination may come from atmospheric particles, pigments, or the leaching of color from a wooden form or element in the work itself. This can be minimized by sealing all wood with polyurethane or Thompson's Water Sealer and by using strainers, storage buckets, fasteners, and screens made only of noncorrosive materials such as plastic, aluminum, or brass.

With some of the water removed, David Merkel adds cotton pulp by hand to a wooden frame set on a plastic grid covered with plastic window screen. Both of these materials are readily available at most lumberyards. (The plastic grid is used as a diffusion grating for fluorescent lighting fixtures.) These layers rest on a support frame that allows air to pass beneath the work. This aids the drainage of water and speeds drying.

The pulp is tapped into the mold. A smoother surface will form on the side in contact with the screen. The top side can be manipulated for added texture.

Two corners of the frame have been hinged. The other two have been joined with a hook and eye. The mold thus is easily disassembled when sheet forming is completed. The same mold can be used immediately for the next sheet.

A large fan is used to speed drying. By using a low-shrinkage pulp like short cotton linter or abaca, these sheets will dry flat with little distortion.

Untitled, *from the series* Secret Ceremonies
*David Merkel, 1979. 36" × 36" × 3". Cast paper
and graphite.*

Once the impressions were formed, she couched
sheets made on a 9″ × 12″ mold onto the dampened
earth. For pulp she used phone books, newspapers,
and scraps, which in the forming process picked up
stones and twigs.

In order to create Framed Calipered Traverse,
Diane Katsiaficas had to learn to drive a tractor.
The tiretracks were the image and mold for her
work.

In order to make the piece stable and durable, she
treated the back with a layer of cheesecloth and liquid adobe stabilizer, which gave the final work a
rubbery quality. It was then rolled up and taken to
her studio, where it was treated with pigments.

Framed Calipered Traverse, *detail.*

Framed Calipered Traverse, *Diane Katsiaficas,*
1980. 9′ × 15′ × 10′. (See color section.)

Let De Boat Walk II, *Joan Hall, 1980. 72" × 56" × 6". Cast, dyed, and painted three-dimensional sculpture.*

Maisi, *Joan Hall, 1981. 22" × 56" × 3". Mixed media.*

Pressing the work with felts speeds the drying, compacts the fibers, and affects the final surface texture.

Impressions are made in the work, other objects are added, and the piece is left to dry with the aid of fans. Later, the finished form is painted and treated with other coloring agents. (See Mosaic in color section.)

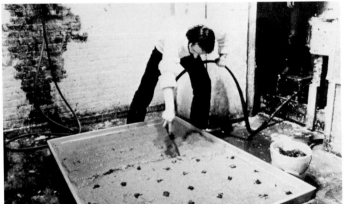

In a collaborative effort at Dieu Donne Press and Paper in New York City, Fredric Amat takes pulp directly from a large ten-pound beater using a hose.

Layers of color are applied, and chunks of other colors are added for texture. The work rests on a plastic screen, which aids drainage and speeds drying.

Piano Trap with Suite of Poems for John Cage, *a performance installation by Coco Gordon, October 25, 1981, London, Ontario. Photograph by Helmut Becker. The structure used in this event was made by pouring cotton rag, flax, and silk pulp over a wire mesh form. These pulps were beaten separately to different stages of hydration in* the Hollander beater and then mixed together. This method of preparing pulp ensured thorough fibrillation yet maintained long fiber length, which was needed because the work could not be pressed. This pulp increased the strength and ensured the stability of the exaggerated forms.

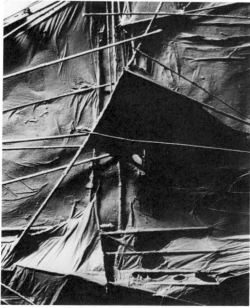

Prairie Ridge Series VIII, *Carol Rosen, 1982.*
Preformed Oriental papers were dampened and
stretched over tall reeds.

Prairie Ridge Series IX *(detail), Carol Rosen,*
1982. The paper became taut upon drying and was
then covered with graphite for color.

Plaster Casting

For hundreds of years plaster has been used to create molds of real objects. It can also be carved. In either case, the absorbent nature of plaster makes it ideal for use in paper casting.

There are many grades of plaster, each for a specific function. Common plaster of paris, available at most hardware stores, can be used for some simple casting projects, but its main function is to patch holes in walls. It is not very absorbent, and the molds made of it will deteriorate after only a few castings have been made. U.S. Gypsum Molding Plaster #1 and Georgia-Pacific K 59 are plasters produced for mold-making and can be purchased at ceramic supply stores. They may be sold under the name of pottery plaster. They are very absorbent, strong, and durable and can be used many times without decomposing or suffering any loss of image detail.

Plaster forms crystals when mixed with water. When added to cold water, the crystals formed are small, producing a tight, dense plaster and a mold with a hard, durable surface. When the plaster is mixed with hot water, the crystals formed are large, producing a mold with a grainy texture.

The proportion of dry material to water is critical for proper crystal formation. Twenty-two ounces of plaster are added to every pound of water. (For convenience, one pint of water equals one pound.) The dry powder is always added to the water, and sifting the powder through a strainer will eliminate lumps in the mixture. Stirring will speed the setting time and produce larger crystals. The longer it takes for plaster to set, the denser and stronger it will be.

When determining the amount of plaster for a specific mold, several formulas may be used. For the volume of a cube, the formula is: Volume equals Length times Width times Height ($V = L \times W \times H$). For example, a box 6 inches high,

Several containers of plaster can be made at one time. Plaster of paris can be used, but pottery plaster is more absorbent and stronger. The setting process will proceed slowly for twenty to thirty minutes as long as cold water is used and the mixture is left unstirred. Stirring and heat both accelerate the setting of the mixture.

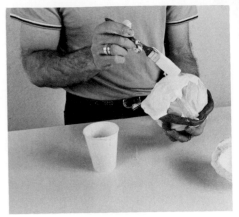

A thin layer of plaster is brushed over the object and the lip formed of plasticene. To prevent the plaster from setting in the brush, an extra container of water should be available for rinsing.

7 inches deep, and 8 inches long contains 336 cubic inches of volume ($V = 6 \times 7 \times 8 = 366$ cubic inches). One quart of water plus 2¾ pounds of plaster will make 80 cubic inches of solid plaster. When converting from cubic inches to quarts, the cubic inches divided by eighty equals the number of quarts of water to be added (cu. in. ÷ 80 = qts. or 336 ÷ 80 = 4.1 quarts).

The following table will help you determine the amount of plaster you will

Water : Plaster Ratio—1 : 1⅜ by weight

Water	Plaster	Water	Plaster
½ pt.	11 oz.	6 qts.	16 lbs. 8 oz.
1 pt.	1 lb. 6 oz.	7 qts.	19 lbs. 4 oz.
1½ pts.	2 lbs. 4 oz.	8 qts.	22 lbs.
1 qt.	2 lbs. 12 oz.	9 qts.	24 lbs. 12 oz.
1½ qts.	4 lbs. 2 oz.	10 qts.	27 lbs. 8 oz.
2 qts.	5 lbs. 8 oz.	11 qts.	30 lbs. 4 oz.
2½ qts.	6 lbs. 14 oz.	12 qts.	33 lbs.
3 qts.	8 lbs. 4 oz.	13 qts.	35 lbs. 12 oz.
3½ qts.	9 lbs. 10 oz.	14 qts.	38 lbs. 8 oz.
4 qts.	11 lbs.	15 qts.	41 lbs. 4 oz.
4½ qts.	12 lbs. 6 oz.		
5 qts.	13 lbs. 12 oz.	For each additional quart beyond	
5½ qts.	15 lbs. 2 oz.	15, add 2 lbs. 12 oz. of plaster.	

Courtesy of Chris Guston.

Pulp can be pressed into an unsealed plaster mold as shown in the upper right. Another method involves laminating thin, lightweight castings like the one shown in the lower right.

Mold release agents are used to prevent objects from sticking to the plaster. In most cases they are water soluble soaps (liquid dish soap will work). A commonly used release agent called green soap can be purchased at ceramic and art supply stores. It needs to be cooked for several hours. The resulting soap is very fine and thin and does not produce bubbles when brushed on the object to be cast. Bubbles can cause pockmarks on the surface of the image.

The main consideration in examining an object to be cast is the awareness of undercuts, any plane on the surface of the object which goes behind another. For example, when casting a round rubber ball, any point beyond the midline will make it impossible to remove the trapped ball from the hardened plaster.

One more word about objects to be cast. Right angles are difficult to remove from a mold. If at all possible, taper the form slightly to aid separation.

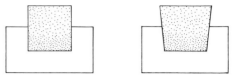

Water is absorbed in a plaster mold, passes through it, and evaporates off its back side. Plaster molds for papermaking do not need to be heavy and thick to do their job well. A thin mold of uniform thickness can be strong, and water will evaporate quickly from it.

need, based on quarts of water. Remember, the proportion of dry material to water is critical. In a situation like the example in which 4.1 quarts of water are needed, use the formula for 4½ quarts of water and throw away the excess; don't guess and add a little more powder or a little less water. One more important point: always use new plaster or plaster that has been stored in plastic bags. It is hydrophilic and pulls water out of the air. This begins the crystallization process while the powder is still in the bag. It will affect your mixing proportions and the setting time of the plaster mixture.

When making large solid molds, hardware cloth (a woven wire mesh with ¼- to ½-inch mesh) can be embedded in the mold for reinforcement.

The object to be cast should be impervious to water (plastic, ceramic, or fruits and vegetables) or made impervious by applying coats of paste or liquid wax, polyurethane, or acrylic spray varnish. Wet clay can be used if it is sealed with spray varnish and then coated with a mold release.

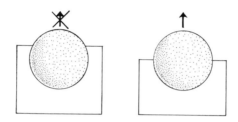

In some cases, undercuts can be incorporated if the object can be removed from the casting at another angle.

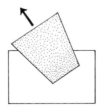

Some forms cannot be cast as a one-piece mold but can be successfully reproduced with a multiple-piece system.

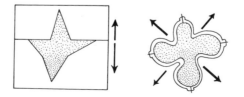

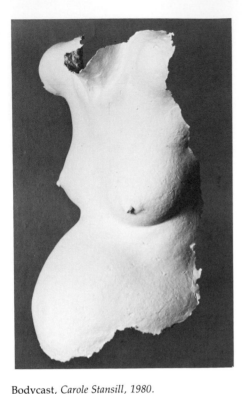

Bodycast, *Carole Stansill, 1980.*

Mary, *Arlene Toonkel. 26″ × 14″ × 5″. Cast paper. Photograph by R. DiLiberto.*

Plasticene, an oil-base clay available at art supply stores, can be pressed against the objects to be cast and used to delineate seam lines. For a one-piece, simple mold, the plaster is then brushed onto the object and the plasticene, which creates a lip for the mold. For small objects, plaster is applied in even layers until the mold is one half inch thick all over. As the plaster sets, heat develops, and the object should not be removed until the mold is cool again, forty minutes or so. At that point, if a multiple-piece mold is to be made, the plasticene can be removed and repositioned for the next section. The edge of the first section should be lightly coated with soap and the next area of plaster brushed in place.

The mold will be completely dry when it no longer feels cool to the touch. At this point, the object can be removed and casting can begin. Once set, a plaster mold is insoluble in water.

Pressing wet pulp directly into the mold will result in a thick, opaque casting. Adding a small amount of adhesive (methylcellulose) to the pulp beforehand will improve its strength. Too much, however, will attach the casting to the mold.

Another approach to casting, laminate casting, involves the layering of small pieces of already formed and lightly pressed paper. These pieces are tapped in place with a stiff bristled brush. Methylcellulose is brushed on the base layer, and the process is repeated until a thin casting is formed. Soaking the mold in cold water for ten minutes before starting prevents the papers from drying out too quickly and allows more time for the laminating process. These techniques may be combined when exotic plant pulps are used for their surface qualities or color and when only small amounts of these pulps are available. A bulkier casting can be produced by laminating the mold with the exotic pulp, then backing it with a more readily available pulp.

Spraying Pulp

Louis Lieberman has modified the procedure for creating castings in plaster molds. His image is created in hard-grade plasticene modeled directly on a Formica surface. Plaster is applied to this image in two layers. A hard plaster is applied directly to the plasticene and forms the durable working surface of the mold. A second layer of plaster whipped full of air by a mixing device is applied on top of the first. Upon drying this second layer will be extremely absorbent and will pull out the large amounts of water sprayed on the mold during the casting process.

For pulp Lieberman uses commercial etching paper that has soaked and aged for several weeks in a refrigerator. This is then mixed in a kitchen blender and added to the chamber of a modified paint spray gun. An air compressor powers the gun and forces the fibers into intimate contact with the mold, producing an extremely smooth surface on the casting.

A modified spray gun is used to apply a thin layer of pulp to the absorbent plaster mold.

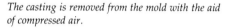

The casting is removed from the mold with the aid of compressed air.

An extremely short-fibered pulp is prepared in the blender.

The resulting paper is very thin.

Untitled, *Louis Lieberman, 1981. 36″ × 36″. Pencil on cast paper. Photograph courtesy of the Harm Bouckaert Gallery, New York.*

To ensure that the casting does not stick to the mold, Lieberman sprays the mold with talc. These thin castings are made more rigid after drying by coating each side with a sizing and applying several coats of gelatin-based gesso to the back. He combines additives, flocking, clay, and powdered dry plaster to the pulp to reduce shrinkage and distortion of the casting while in the mold and to give the sheet the proper tooth or texture needed to make the dark pencil lines of his images.

This technique can be modified to produce papers without molds. Artist Joe Zina sprays colored pulps onto a taut bed sheet to create large, colorful and lightweight papers. These are then shaped into forms, or the paper is torn and used collage-style for two-dimensional wall works. His sprayer is a gun used for spraying concrete. Because of its large orifice, some long-fibered pulps can be sprayed.

First Mist, *Joe Zina, 1982. 4' × 5'. Sprayed, dyed pulp.*
First Mist (*detail*).

Rubber Molds

An object with undercuts cannot be cast in a one-piece plaster mold, but it can be successfully cast in a mold made of latex rubber (natural rubber). Its flexible nature allows latex rubber to be stretched and pulled away from the object and from the dried paper casting.

The process of making a latex mold is more time-consuming but no more difficult than making a plaster mold. Several thin layers of latex (available at many art supply stores) should be brushed on the object and allowed to dry completely—twelve to twenty-four hours. Fine wood dust from a sanding machine can be mixed with latex in the next layers to make them thicker and speed the building up of the mold. If the mold is to undergo extreme stretching, it should be reinforced with a layer of cheesecloth between layers of latex. When dry, the latex will detach easily from the model without a separating agent.

Before you remove the mold from the object, a support mold of plaster should be made to hold the flexible latex mold during casting and storing. The plaster is brushed on the back of the latex mold and when dry can be separated.

Latex rubber molds should be stored in a cool, dry place. They do not last long, becoming dry, brittle, and easily torn within a year. Storing them in their plaster support mold is essential to maintain their original shape.

Silicone rubber is a long-lasting synthetic and quite expensive. It is available through the Dow Corning Chemical Co. One advantage of this material is that it can be poured over an object to create a mold of any thickness. It cures in only a few hours. Only a single application is needed. The release agent is dish soap that has been allowed to dry on the object. The tough, durable mold will stretch to release undercuts. Silicone rubber molds also should be backed with a plaster mold for support.

Lynn Forgach of Exeter Press and Paper in New York shows a latex mold used to form the head of Bust with Shells *by Peter Saari.*

The latex mold rests in a plaster support mold held together with rubber bands and nails.

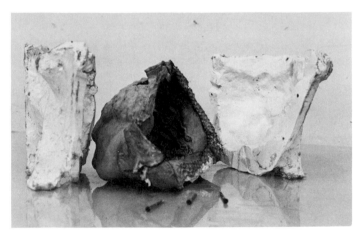

When the bands and nails are removed, the latex mold comes out.

To produce the casting, the pulp is pressed into the mold to form a casting approximately one inch thick.

When dry, the final casting is ready for use in the work.

Bust with Shells, *Peter Saari, 1981. Acrylic, plaster, canvas, wood, paper pulp.*

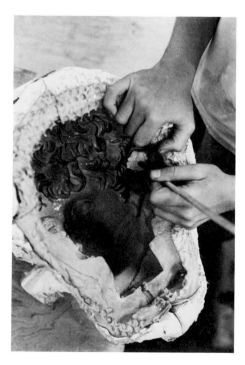

Shaped Molds

These highly refined molds were built by Winifred Lutz for producing three-dimensional artworks. They are based on the idea of mold-making as the direct process for image-making. They are designed to be used with the Oriental sheet-forming process using gampi, ramie, linen, and bast fiber from indigenous plants and neri or its synthetic substitute. The resulting images are thin and translucent, emphasizing the character of each fiber.

Inherent in the success of these castings is a thorough understanding of and familiarity with a wide range of fiber types and their preparation. Depending on how fibers are prepared, each has a specific color, density, sheen, shrinkage rate, and fiber length. An understanding of these variables increases the visual possibilities of the casting and guarantees its success.

Fibers are carefully prepared by cooking, retting, or simple washing to ensure that the final paper is clear of lignin and other impurities. The fibers are then beaten in a stamper beater or in a carefully controlled Hollander beater to ensure that fiber length is maintained for strength and a particular surface quality and density.

Shaped brass screening is sewn to wooden frames. These sections are attached to each other with brass screws and wooden clips. The paper casting is formed nagashizuki style. Photographs courtesy of Winifred Lutz.

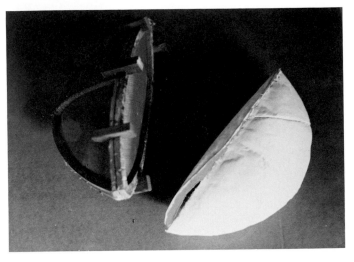

Pulp and neri are poured into the mold and distributed over the surfaces. The casting is allowed to dry in the mold, and the sections are then disassembled to reveal the totally three-dimensional translucent form. This casting is made of ramie beaten nine hours.

This fabric screen mold has a very high deckle to ensure the complete covering of the ridge on the image. The finished casting (left) is made of ramie fiber by the nagashizuki method.

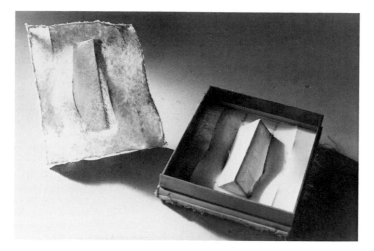

The cloth surface is tied to the frame with waxed linen cord, a very time-consuming process. The cast image is allowed to dry on the mold. The cloth is then untied from the frame and pulled gently away from the casting.

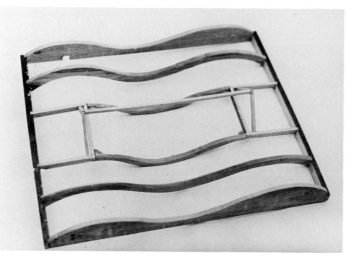

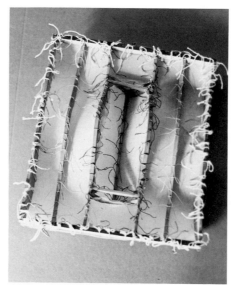

This shaped frame has been designed to support a removable cotton cloth surface on which the paper will be formed.

Deckle Box

A very deep deckle attached to a mold can be floated in the vat. Pulps can be poured into this frame and shaken to align the fibers and produce extremely thick sheets or special marbled effects. When removed from the water and allowed to drain, the deckle can be taken off and the sheet couched onto the felt. Since pulp is poured directly into the mold, this method is also useful when only a small amount of pulp is available.

This deckle box is attached to the frame with metal fasteners and has handles for easy lifting.

1

The pulp is poured into it as it rests in a vat of water.

2

5
The deckle is removed to reveal the thick sheet.

6
Some of the excess water is removed with sponges.

The pulp is distributed by hand.

3

The deckle box is removed from the water and allowed to drain.

4

7

It is then couched directly onto the back of a latex mold.

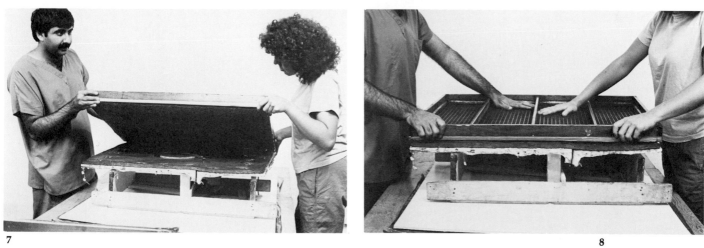

8

The sheet is then pressed.

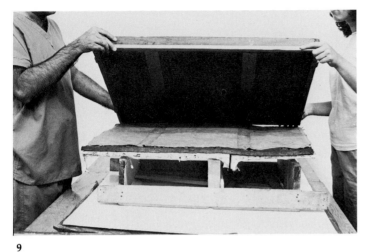

9
The mold is removed from the sheet.

10
The sheet is pressed again.

11
Two works by Cynthia Carlson, Fleur-de-lis *and* Loop, *1981. Published by 724 Prints and produced at Exeter Press, New York. The images were formed in latex molds and backed with thick sheets formed in a deckle box. The work was then painted.*

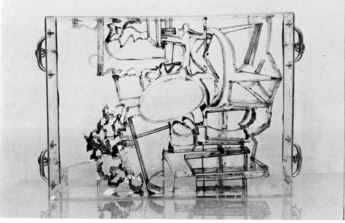

1
A more complicated deckle box was made for the production of Living Room Diptych *by Cham Hendon. It was made from metal and plexiglass at Exeter Press.*

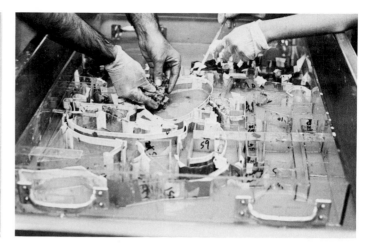

2
Into each area, colored pulps are placed and mixed to produce swirls of color.

3
With the deckle box removed, the thick pulp areas are ready to be couched.

5 *The mold is pressed and then pressed again in the hydraulic press.*

4
The mold is tipped.

Living Room Diptych, *Cham Hendon, 1982. 44"*
× 30". Manila hemp and pigment. Photographs of
the production of this artwork are by Lynn
Forgach.

Vacuum Table Casting

Generally, three-dimensional objects cannot be pressed in a papermaker's press because of their high relief. At other times, fragile elements embedded in a work prevent traditional pressing, or the limited size of the press does not allow larger pieces to be pressed. For these occasions and for other uses, a vacuum table is a useful piece of studio equipment.

Designed by California artists Harold Paris and Charles Hilger, it consists of a flat surface attached to a vacuum chamber, a vacuum pump, and a water storage tank. A vacuum table is relatively easy to make using a wet and dry vacuum cleaner available at most hardware stores and lumberyards. Commercial tables are available as well and are much quieter and more durable than those run by a vacuum cleaner.

The surface of the table is drilled with small holes every six inches, but this distance does not seem to be critical and can be increased. The holes feed into a vacuum chamber, which can be simply a space under the table. All of the seams of this enclosure should be caulked with silicone sealer to ensure an airtight seal. Through a hole in the bottom of the chamber a vacuum hose is attached. The top of the table should be covered with several layers of flexible plastic screening, and a felt, on which the artwork is formed, should be placed on top of the screening.

Once the image is created, the entire surface of the table is covered with thin plastic sheeting, which will seal all of the air holes and create a vacuum within the box once the pump has been turned on. The extracted water travels beneath the felt, through the space created by the screen, through the small holes, and into the vacuum chamber. After several minutes, the pump can be turned off. The image will require further drying, but a great percentage of water is removed by this process.

Because of its structure, polystyrene plastic can be used as a mold on the vacuum table. Sheet-formed papers or pulp can be placed on top of this Styrofoam image. Water extracted by the vacuum will be pulled through the foam, partially drying and adhering the pulp to the mold. This table can be used to pull excess water from plaster molds, as well.

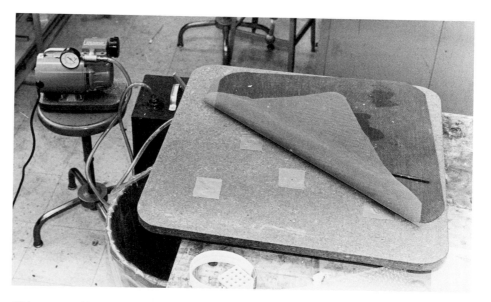

This vacuum table was produced by Charles Hilger. It consists of a vacuum pump, a water storage tank, and a table surface covered with two layers of flexible mesh.

A piece of wood restrains additional pulp poured over the sheet for added thickness.

2

1
Elaine Koretsky demonstrates one of the uses of the Hilger vacuum table. A basketry mat is placed on a white felt, and a freshly made unpressed sheet of paper is placed over it.

4
Thin plastic is placed over the surface of the paper and the table. Here you can see the contours of the mat as the pulp is flattened by the vacuum's pressure. After several minutes, most of the water will be removed from the object. It is then uncovered and left to air dry. Once dry, the undamaged mat can be removed.

Colored pulp is applied freehand for decorative effects.

3

A variation on the Hilger vacuum table can be made using two layers of marine plywood held apart by a 2″ × 4″ wooden frame. The top layer has holes drilled every six inches for the removal of water. To the bottom of this box is attached a wet and dry vacuum cleaner. All of the edges of this frame have been sealed with silicone sealer to ensure a proper vacuum.

6

5

The surface of the table is covered with two layers of flexible screen. These create a space below the white felt and paper object. Water travels from the casting through this space into small holes that carry it to a holding tank.

7

Untitled, *Charles Hinman, 1980. 22" × 28". Cast pigmented paper formed on a vacuum table.*

Untitled, *Charles Hinman. 22" × 28". Cast pigmented paper formed on a vacuum table.*

Red River Series #2, *White Edition, Gregg Lefevre, 1980. 30" × 20". Cast paper.*

6 | Glossary

adhere
To bind the surfaces of unlike materials.

aging, syneresis
Condition in which similar particles have a greater attraction to themselves than to absorbed water and pull together with time. Thus, an aged sheet is more dense and dimensionally stable than a newly formed sheet.

archival paper
Paper with a pH of 7.0. Paper conservationists suggest that contemporary papers be produced with a residual buffer content of between two and three percent to counteract future acidic contamination due to printing processes, improper storage or environmental pollution.

bast fiber
Fibers derived from the phloem of inner bark of plants. Flax, hemp, jute, ramie, mitsumata, gampi, and kozo are typical bast fiber plants.

beating
The physical or mechanical process that separates fibrous elements from each other and causes internal and external splitting, or fibrillation, and softening of the fibers.

black bark
The outer, brittle layer of a bast fiber plant, usually removed to reveal lighter-colored, more flexible underlayers.

bleed
The leaching of color from a pulp of a pigmented object. In relation to dyes and pigments, it is the excess amount of unbonded colorant that runs from the pulp during rinsing.

buffer
A substance that reduces the effect of another substance. Calcium carbonate and magnesium carbonate are two base chemicals that reduce the effect of acidic chemicals.

cellulose
A molecular glucose chain of up to 5,000 units and the most plentiful carbohydrate produced by plants.

cellulose fiber
Fiber derived from plants. Examples of cellulose fibers are cotton, linen, hemp, jute, and ramie. Viscose rayon is a synthetic cellulosic fiber.

cohere
To bind the surfaces of like materials without use of a cementing substance.

cotton linters
The coarser, shorter fibers that remain attached to the cotton seed after the long fibers have been removed for textile use. Linters are cut from the seed, cooked, and used in the paper industry. They produce a low-shrinkage pulp that is good for bulk casting. Their fiber length is too short for making durable book papers.

couching
The process of transferring a freshly made sheet of paper from the mold onto another surface, such as a felt or another fresh sheet of paper. Double couching involves pressing one fresh sheet onto another fresh sheet. Pressing will bond these layers together.

deckle
A wood frame that rests on or is hinged to the mold. It contains the pulp on the screen during sheet formation and defines the edges of the sheet; thus the term deckled edge.

dimensional stability
The degree to which a sheet changes due to rewetting or pressing. This is affected greatly by the drying process.

durability
The degree to which paper retains its original qualities under continual use.

dyes
Soluble chemicals that bond with the surface of a fiber and color it. Dyes are widely used in the textile industry because they do not affect the texture or "feel" of the cloth.

felts
A general name for the cloth placed between wet sheets during the couching process. These can be wool or synthetic and act as spacers, which provide channels for the rapid removal of water during pressing.

fiber
In papermaking, the slender, threadlike cellulose structure that coheres with others to form a sheet.

fibrillation
The internal and external splitting of the fiber that results from beating.

fibrils
The hairlike structures, produced by the beating process, on the surface and within cellulose fibers. They are the most active sites of hydrogen bonding in papermaking.

filler
A general term for materials added to the pulp to give the finished sheet a smoother surface or greater density. Usually nonoxidizing clays or minerals.

freeness
The drainage rate or flow of water away from the pulp during sheet forming.

gampi
Wikstroemia cannescens. A Japanese fiber that produces tough, thin, glossy paper.

green bark
With reference to Oriental bast fibers, it is the layer below the black, outer bark and contains a bitter chemical that repels insects.

half stuff
A general expression for partially prepared pulp. It usually refers to cut, cooked, and partially beaten rag.

hemicellulose
Pentose and hexose sugar chains; also known as gammacellulose. A small percentage is recommended in a pulp mixture because it is more hydrophilic than cellulose and thus makes the pulp more susceptible to beating.

Hollander beater
The traditional piece of equipment in European-style papermaking for the beating and hydrating of fibers prior to sheet forming.

hydrogen bonding
The electronic bonding of adjacent atoms within and between the fibers and fibrils of the pulp that, along with friction and interlocking, hold the sheet together and give it strength.

hydrophilic
Water-loving. This characteristic of cellulose fiber makes it very susceptible to separation by beating.

hydrophobic
Water-fearing. The intercellular cement in plants, lignin, is hydrophobic. It remains unaffected by the passage of water through the plant and consequently is successful at holding the plant together. Sizing compounds when dry are said to be hydrophobic.

hydropulper
A mixing device used to stir pulp. It can be used to separate some linter pulps but does not hydrate or beat the fibers.

Indian hemp
Crotolaria juncca. Long-fibered, opaque pulp.

kozo
General term for a variety of papermaking mulberries. An example is *Broussonetia papyrifera,* which is characterized by strong, sinewy, long fibers.

laid paper
Paper formed on a laid-line screen.

Lightnin' mixer
The brand name of a stirring device used to mix pulp.

lignin
A hydrophobic component of plants that tends to decrease interfiber bonding in paper. It is sometimes referred to as an intercellular cement. Lignins are removed by cooking in a caustic solution or by bleaching.

linters
A general term for preprocessed pulp that can be purchased in either sheet or chip form. Examples are cotton, wood, and abaca linters.

lye
Caustic soda, or sodium hydroxide, a strong caustic used to cook fibers.

Manila hemp
Abaca, a variety of banana plant (*Musa textilis*), that produces long-fibered, lustrous, relatively transparent paper. When purchased precooked in sheet or chip form, it can be easily broken down in the Lightnin' mixer or kitchen blender.

mitsumata
Bast fiber shrub of the Thymelaeceae family characterized by fine-grained, soft, absorbent, and slightly lustrous fibers.

mold
A wooden frame covered with a surface on which paper is formed. In European tradition, this surface is either a woven wire cloth or a laid-line screen supported from beneath by a system of pine ribs. In Oriental tradition, it is a flexible bamboo or reed mat that rests on a wooden frame. Molds are usually accompanied by an additional wooden frame, the deckle.

nagashi-zuki
Oriental-style discharge papermaking using neri.

neri
A general term for the various kinds of vegetable mucilage used in Oriental papermaking as an aid during sheet forming. Usually found in the roots of plants in the mallow family and the inner bark of plants in the saxifrage family. In Oriental tradition, neri comes from tororo-aoi (*Hibiscus manihot*).

papyrus
A prepaper substrate made of layers of a nonwoody aquatic reed. The word "paper" is derived from this Greek word.

pectin
A polysaccharide contained in flax. It is responsible for the oily look of some papers made of uncooked flax.

permanence
The degree to which paper resists chemical action that may result from impurities in the paper itself or agents from the surrounding atmosphere.

pH
Denotes the acidity or alkalinity of a substance. Zero to 7 indicates an acid condition; 7 to 14 indicates an alkaline condition; 7 is neutral.

pigment
A dry substance, usually pulverized, that remains insoluble when mixed with water. Pigments are derived from organic and inorganic sources.

post
A stack of newly formed wet sheets and felts.

protein fiber
Fiber derived from animals. Examples are wool, silk, hair. Nylon is a synthetic protein fiber.

pulp
A general term for the substance that paper is made from; beaten fiber and water.

rag
A general term for old or new cotton or linen cloth used for pulp. New rag refers to cuttings from the textile industry. Old rag is cloth that has already been used as a textile; for example, bed sheets, tablecloths, shirts, and dresses. Rag pulps are composed of the longest fibers of the cotton and linen plant and make strong, durable papers.

retting
Exposing plant fibers to moisture and bacterial activity. This process begins the breakdown of the noncellulose constituents of the plant, thereby loosening the fibers and preparing them for further processing. Flax or other bast fibers usually undergo retting. A slow cooking process.

rice paper
A misnomer for Oriental and especially Japanese handmade papers. The original "rice paper" is a paperlike substance sliced from the pith of the Taiwanese tree *Aracia papyrifera.*

shukushi
Japanese term for recycled paper.

sisal
Agave sisalina. A leaf fiber similar to Indian hemp.

size, sizing
A general term for products that act as a barrier around the fibers. They decrease the absorbency of the paper and act as an adhesive to strengthen the sheet. They can be synthetic (Aquapel or Hercon), animal (rabbit skin glue), or vegetable (potato starch).

su
A flexible screen usually of bamboo, and sometimes reed, used in Japanese papermaking. It rests on the frame and is the surface on which the sheet of paper is formed.

tororo-aoi
Hibiscus manihot. The roots of this plant are crushed and soaked in water to make the most common kind of neri mucilage used in Oriental papermaking.

true hemp
Cannabis sativa.

washing soda
Sodium carbonate, a caustic used for cooking plant fiber.

water leaf
Unsized paper.

watermark
A design applied to the surface of the mold or formed in the mold that produces a tonal image in the resulting sheet where more or less pulp is distributed.

wetting agent
A substance that speeds the penetration of liquid into dry powder or fiber. Examples are dishwashing soap, denatured alcohol, and gum arabic.

white bark
The light-colored inner layer of bast fiber used to make the whitest paper.

wood ash
Potassium carbonate. A mild caustic used for cooking fibers and derived from burned plant material. It is soaked in water and drained. This water contains dissolved alkalies and is used to cook the fiber.

woven paper
Smooth paper made on a European mold with a woven wire surface.

Appendix

Ibis Paper Works
1520 Las Palomas Dr.
La Habra Heights, CA 90631
Collaboration mill and teaching facility

Jabberwock
GPO Box 2520
Hobart, Tasmania 7001
Australia
Custom papermill

Jinn Handmade Paper
Nebenstrasse 9
636 Friedberg 6
West Germany
Custom papermill

Kalamazoo Handmade Papers
5947 North 25th St.
Kalamazoo, MI 49004
Production papermill specializing in Oriental
paper

Kensington Paper Mill
2527 Magnolia St.
Oakland, CA 94607
Custom paper and collaboration mill and
etching studio

La Papeterie St. Armand
110 rue Young
Montreal, Quebec H3C 2E7
Canada
Custom papermill

Liliaceae Press
1970 S. Davis St.
McMinnville, OR 97128
Publisher (*Plant Fibers for Papermaking* by Bell)
with traveling workshops

Lullwater Papermill
3121 White Oak St.
Thomson, GA 30824
Production papermill

Massachusetts Handmade Paper
11 Woodbridge St.
North Cambridge, MA 02140
Custom papermill

Mould and Deckle Paper Mill
221 Canterbury Rd.
Heathmont, Victoria 3135
Australia
Teaching facility and custom mill specializing
in recycling

Oak Park Press and Papermill
1233 N. River Blvd.
Wichita, KS 67203
Custom papermill

Oikofugic Editions
Cleveland Institute of Art
18414 Lynton Rd.
Cleveland, OH 44122
Collaborative book works and custom
papermill

Old Harrie's Shed
General Delivery
Ketch Harbor, N.S. B0J 1X0
Canada
Collaboration and production papermill

The Paper Mill, Artists
Resource Center
800 Traction Ave.
Los Angeles, CA 90013
Educational facility

The Papier Farm
10351 N. Cedarburg Rd.
Mequon, WI 53092
Custom papermill and teaching facility

Papyrus Institute
3 Nile Ave., P.O. Box 45 Orman
Cairo, Egypt
Papyrus production mill and educational
facility

Beverly Plummer, Papermaker
RR 5, Box 234
Burnsville, NC 28714
Production papermill with traveling work-
shops

The Prints and the Pulper
1020 Côllege Ave.
Racine, WI 53403
Custom papermill and educational facility

Raggidy Andy Papermill
3800 N. Fairfax Dr. #612
Arlington, VA 22203
Production papermill and supplier

Rugg Road Handmade Papers
40 Rugg Road
Allston, MA 02134
Custom papermill, collaboration and teaching
facility

Sandbar Willow Mill
2468 S. 3rd St. Plaza
Omaha, NE 68108
Custom papermill

Sea Pen Press and Paper Mill
2900 21st Ave. South
Seattle, WA 98144
Limited edition book publisher, custom
papermill

Silo Paper
Box 171, RD 1
Eagle Bridge, NY 12057
Custom papermill, collaboration facility

Singing Bone Press
228 Edgar Rd.
St. Louis, MO 63119
Custom papermill, collaboration facility

Terrapin Papermill
2318 Nicholson St.
Cincinnati, OH 45211
Production papermill, letterpress printer, collaboration facility

Trout Paper
Box #174, RD #1
Eagle Bridge, NY 12057
Collaboration mill

Twinrocker Paper Co.
RFD 2
Brookston, IN 47923
Production paper and collaboration mill with
workshops and supplies

Uncle Bob Leslie Papermill
c/o Joyce Schmidt
Moshe Shapira 21
Netanya, Israel
Educational facility

Michael John Verlangieri
790 Santa Barbara Dr.
Claremont, CA 91711
Production papermill and supplier

Waterleaf Mill
c/o Apartado Postal #96
San Miguel de Allende 37700
Guanajuato, Mexico 21564
Production papermill

Watermark Paper and Press
Coco Gordon, Director
175 East Shore Rd.
Huntington Bay, NY 11743
Custom papermill and collaboration facility

Paper and Papermaking Equipment Suppliers

The following suppliers all carry products that can be used by the hand papermaker. It is not possible to list all of the sources for some supplies, as some are quite common. Consult your phone book for certain local distributors.

Beaters

Davis Hodges Hollander Beater
Colorado Instrument
2200 Central Ave., Suite E
Boulder, CO 80301

Oak Park Press and Papermill
1233 North River Blvd.
Wichita, KS 67203
Hollander and Umpherston beaters, rolls, and bedplates

Art Schade
P.O. Box 257
Village Station
New York, NY 10014
Custom beaters only

Twinrocker Equipment Co.
110 3rd St.
P.O. Box 246
Brookston, IN 47923
Beaters and presses

Voith-Allis
P.O. Box 2337
Appleton, WI 54911
Valley beaters

Dyes and Pigments

Fezandie and Sperrle
111 8th Ave.
New York, NY 10011
Dry pigment

Mobay Chemical Corp.
Dyestuff Division
P.O. Box 385
Union Metropolitan Park
Union, NJ 07083
Dyes, water-dispersed pigments, retention agents

Pro Chemical and Dye, Inc.
P.O. Box 14
Somerset, MA 02726

Procion dye
Pylam Products, Inc.
95-10 218th St.
Queens Village, NY 11429
Direct dyes, fiber reactive dyes

Straw Into Gold
5533 College Ave.
Oakland, CA 94618
Dyes, natural dyestuffs

Felts

Appleton Mills
P.O. Box 1899
Appleton, WI 54913
Felts

Lee Scott McDonald
P.O. Box 264
Charlestown, MA 02129

Molds

E. Amies and Sons
c/o Barcham Green & Co., Ltd.
Hayle Mill
Maidstone
Kent, ME 15 6XQ
England
Traditional European molds

Cooper/Taylor Molds, Ltd.
18414 Lynton Rd.
Cleveland, OH 44122
Mold kits

Lee Scott McDonald
P.O. Box 264
Charlestown, MA 02129
Oriental and European molds, felts, fibers, formation aids, everything for the hand papermaker

Asao Shimura
Cannabis Press
431 Fukuhara Kasama-shi
Ibaragi-ken 309-15
Japan
Sells Oriental fibers and molds; offers workshops and lectures

Presses

Atlantic Paperworks
104 Benevolent St.
Providence, RI 02906
Hydraulic presses

Ibis Paperworks
1520 Las Palomas Dr.
La Habra Heights, CA 90631
Hydraulic presses

Twinrocker Equipment Co.
110 3rd St.
P.O. Box 246
Brookston, IN 47923
Hydraulic presses

Pulp

Buckeye Cellulose Corp.
P.O. Box 8407
Memphis, TN 38108
Cotton pulp

Carriage House Handmade Paper Works
8 Evans Rd.
Brookline, MA 02146
Abaca and other processed pulps

Cheney Pulp and Paper Co.
P.O. Box 60
Franklin, OH 45005
Rag pulp. 250-pound minimum order

Dieu Donne Press and Paper
3 Crosby St.
New York, NY 10013
Cotton and linen rag, cotton linter, wet or dried pulps

Gold's Art and Frame Shop
406 N. Chestnut St.
Lumberton, NC 28358
Distributor for Alpha Cellulose cotton linters on East Coast

Kensington Paper Mill
2527 Magnolia St.
Oakland, CA 94607

Lee Scott McDonald
P.O. Box 264
Charlestown, MA 02129
Oriental and European fibers

Twinrocker Paper Co.
RFD 2
Brookston, IN 47923

Michael John Verlangieri
790 Santa Barbara Dr.
Claremont, CA 91711
Distributor for Alpha Cellulose cotton linters on West Coast

Wire Cloth

Sinclair Co.
60 Appleton St.
Holyoke, MA 10140
Laid-line wire

H. M. Spencer
78 N. Canal St.
Holyoke, MA 10140
Laid-line wire

Frank Davis Co.
P.O. Box 231
Cambridge, MA 02139
Used equipment

80 Papers
80 Thompson St.
New York, NY 10013
Sells handmade paper

James F. Gormely
Converting & Paper Mill Consultants
7072 Spier Falls Rd., No. 1
Gansevoort, NY 12813
Used equipment

Len Hartnett
Archival Products, Inc.
300 N. Quidnessett Rd.
North Kingstown, RI 02852
Archival supplies

Chuck Hilger
705 Pacific
Santa Cruz, CA 95060
Vacuum tables

Mixing Equipment Co., Inc.
216 Mt. Read Blvd.
Rochester, NY 14603
"Lightnin' mixers"

New York Central Art Supply Co.
62 Third Ave.
New York, NY 10013
Handmade paper

Dan Smith Inks
1111 W. Nickerson St.
Seattle, WA 98119
Handmade papers

Talas Division of Technical Library Service
105 Fifth Ave.
New York, NY 10011
Archival materials, handmade paper, and
sizing

Twinrocker Paper Co.
RFD 2
Brookston, IN 47923
Books, pulps, sizing, molds, instruction,
everything for the hand papermaker

Wei T'o Associates, Inc.
P.O. Drawer 40
Matteson, IL 60443
Deacidification solutions and sprays

Metric Conversions

Metric Weight

1 gram = 15.43 grains
10 grams = .35 ounce
100 grams = 3.5 ounces
1,000 grams = 1 kilogram = 2.2 pounds

Metric Fluid Capacity

10 milliliters = 1 centiliter = .338 fluid ounce
100 milliliters = 1 deciliter = 3.38 fluid ounces
1,000 milliliters = 1 liter = 1.05 liquid quarts
10 liters = 2.64 gallons

Avoirdupois Weight

1 ounce = 28 grams
16 ounces = 1 pound = 453.5 grams

Liquid Measure

16 fluid ounces = 1 pint = 0.47 liter
2 pints = 1 quart = .95 liter
4 quarts = 1 gallon = 3.79 liters

Bibliography

Adams, Alice. "Douglass Howell." *Craft Horizons* 22 (September 1962):26–29.

Adrosko, Rita J. *Natural Dyes and Home Dyeing*. New York: Dover Publications, 1971.

Ainsworth, J. H. *Paper, The Fifth Wonder*. Kaukauna, Wisc.: Thomas Printing and Publishing Co., Ltd., 1959.

American Paper and Pulp Association. *The Dictionary of Paper, Including Pulp, Paperboard, Paper Properties and Related Terms*. 3rd ed. New York City, 1965.

American Paper Institute. *How You Can Make Paper*. New York,

Barrett, Timothy. *Nagashizuki, The Japanese Craft of Hand Papermaking*. North Hills, Pa.: Bird and Bull Press, 1979. A limited edition book. A wonderful story about the "feel" of nagashizuki and an informative text.

Barrow, W. J. *Manuscripts and Documents: Their Deterioration and Restoration*.Charlottesville: University of Virginia Press, 1955.

Bell, Lilian. *Plant Fibers for Papermaking*. McMinnville, Ore.: Liliaceae Press, 1981. An exceptional reference work for those interested in local plants.

Browning, B. L. *Analysis of Paper*. New York: Marcel Dekker, Inc., 1977.

Carpenter, Chas. H., and Lawrence, Laney. *Papermaking Fibers*. College of Environmental Science and Forestry, State University of New York, Syracuse, 1952.

Clapp, Anne. *Curatorial Care of Works of Art on Paper*. Intermuseum Conservation Association, Oberlin, Ohio, 1973.

Clark, James d'A. *Pulp Technology and Treatment for Paper*. San Francisco: Miller Freeman Publications, 1978. An excellent text for those with some chemistry background.

Colour Index. London: The Society of Dyers and Colourists, 1956.

Diderot, Denis. *A Diderot Pictorial Encyclopedia of Trades and Industry*. Vol. 2. New York: Dover Publications, 1959. Illustrations of historic mills and processes.

Dye Plants and Dyeing. Vol. 20, no. 3. Brooklyn: Brooklyn Botanical Gardens. A basic dye book.

Fabri, Ralph. *Color*. New York: Watson-Guptill, 1970.

Grae, Ida. *Nature's Colors: Dyes from Plants*. New York: Macmillan Publishing Co., 1979.

Green, J. Barcham. *One Hundred and Fifty Years of Papermaking by Hand*. Maidstone, England: J. Barcham Green, 1967.

Grummer, Arnold. *Paper by Kids*. Minneapolis: Dillon Press, 1980. An excellent introductory book for all levels.

Heller, Jules. *Papermaking*. New York: Watson-Guptill, 1978.

Higham, Robert R. A. *A Handbook of Papermaking*. London: Business Books Ltd., 1968. A good fiber section. Mainly geared to industry.

Hockney, David. *Paper Pools*. New York: Abrams, Inc., 1980. An inspirational art book about contemporary paper.

Hughes, Sukey. *Washi: The World of Japanese Paper*. Tokyo, New York, San Francisco: Kodansha International, 1978. A beautiful tabletop book with many photographs of processes.

Hunter, Dard. *My Life with Paper, An Autobiography*. New York: Alfred Knopf, Inc., 1958.

Hunter, Dard. *Papermaking in Pioneer America*. Philadelphia: University of Pennsylvania Press, 1952.

Hunter, Dard. *Papermaking, The History and Technique of an Ancient Craft*. New York: Dover Books, 1978. An excellent overview and basic reference book.

Isenberg, Irving H. *Papermaking Fibers*. Reprinted from *Economic Botany*, vol. 10, no. 2, April–June 1956.

Ittens, Johannes. *The Art of Color*. New York: Van Nostrand Reinhold Co., 1973. Excellent on color theory.

Johnson, Fridolf. "Henry Morris: Papermaker and Printer." *American Artist* 31 (October 1967):56–61.

Jugaku, Bunsho. *Papermaking by Hand in Japan*. Tokyo: Meiji Shobo, Ltd., 1959.

Koretsky, Elaine. *Color for the Hand Papermaker*. Brookline, Mass.: Carriage House Press and Paper Works, 1982. A necessity for those using color.

Kume, Yasuo. *Tesuki Washi Shuho* (Fine handmade papers of Japan). Tokyo: Yushodo Booksellers Ltd., 1975. Three volumes; 207 assorted samples of washi.

Kunisaki, Jihei, and Kamisuki, Chōhōki. *A Handy Guide to Papermaking After the Japanese*. Translated by Charles Hamilton. Berkeley Book Arts Club, University of California, 1978.

La Français de Lalande, Joseph Jerome. *The Art of Papermaking*. Clare, Ireland: Ashling Press, 1976. Limited edition.

Lockwood's Directory of the Paper and Allied Trades. 49 W. 45th St., New York, N.Y. 10036. Published yearly.

Mason, John. *Papermaking as an Artistic Craft*. London: Faber and Faber, 1959. An excellent introduction; full of wit and information.

Metcalf, H. *Pioneer Book of Nature Crafts* (formerly *Whittlin', Whistlin' and Thing A Majigs*). Citadel Press, 1976. Contais an excellent chapter on preparing tree fiber for cordage.

Morris, Henry. *The Bird and Bull Commonplace Book*. North Hills, Pa.: Bird and Bull Press, 1971. Limited edition.

Morris, Henry. *Omnibus*. North Hills, Pa.: Bird and Bull Press, 1967. Limited edition, University Microfilms, Ann Arbor, Michigan.

Pan, Dr. *Handmade Papers of the World*. Tokyo: Takeo Co., Ltd., 1980.

The Papermaker. Wilmington, Del.: Hercules Co. An in-house magazine available in some libraries. See articles by Harrison Elliot, W. B. Wheelwright, and Henk Vorn.

Papermaking, Art and Craft. New York: American Paper Institute, 1968. An excellent catalogue from an early show.

Parham, R. A., Kaustinen. *Papermaking Materials, an Atlas of Electron Micrographs*. Appleton, Wisc.: Institute of Paper Chemistry, 1974.

Patton, Temple C. *Pigment Handbook*. New York: John Wiley & Sons, 1973.

Phillips' Paper Trade Directory of the World. London: S. C. Phillips & Co., Ltd. Published annually.

Phillpotts, Eden. *Storm in a Teacup*. London: 1919. A novel that takes place in a papermill. One chapter is entitled "Tragedy in the Sizing Room."

Plummer, Beverly. *Earth Presents*. New York: Atheneum, 1974. Paperback by A & W Visuals, New York, 1977. Includes a chapter on papermaking.

Poyser, James Norman. *Experiments in Making Paper by Hand*. Pointe Claire, P.Q., Canada, 1975. Available from author.

Pulp and Paper. San Francisco: Freeman Publications. A directory published annually.

Pulp and Paper Canada. Westmount, P.Q.: National Business Publications Ltd. Published annually. A directory of paper mills and suppliers.

Sarjeant, Peter T. *Handmade Papermaking Manual*. Covington, Va.: Paper Make, 1974.

Shurtleff, William, and Aoyagi, A. *The Book of Kudzu, A Culinary and Healing Guide*. Brookline, Mass.: Autumn Press, 1978. A very good chapter on fiber preparation.

Sommar, Helen. *A Brief Guide to Sources of Fiber and Textile Information*. Washington, D.C.: Information Resources Press, 1973.

Stedman, Ebenezer Hiram. *Bluegrass Craftsman, Being the Reminiscence of Ebenezer Hiram Stedman*. Lexington, Ky.: University of Kentucky Press, 1959. A homey tale of how Stedman made paper.

Studely, Vance. *The Art and Craft of Handmade Paper*. New York: Van Nostrand Reinhold Co., 1977.

Tindale, Thomas and Harriet. *The Handmade Papers of Japan, The Seki Collection*. Rutland, Vt.; Tokyo, Japan: Chas. Tuttle Co., 1952. Can be located in some libraries; a wonderful way to spend many afternoons.

Von Hagen, Victor. *The Aztec and Maya Papermakers*. New York: J. J. Augustin, 1944.

Weeks, Lyman Horace. *History of Papermaking in the United States*. New York: Burt Franklin, 1970 reproduction of 1916 text.

Weygand, James Lamar. *The Weygand Tightwad Beater: Its Design and Construction*. The Private Press of the Indiana Kid, 1970.

Wheelwright, William Bond. *Practical Paper Technology*. Cambridge, Mass.: M. J. & W. B. Wheelwright, Pub., 1951.

Index